KIDS COOK!

GOOD
HOUSEKEEPING

KIDS COOK!

100+ SUPER-EASY, DELICIOUS RECIPES

HEARST
books

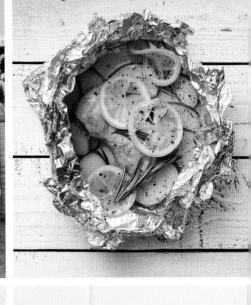

CONTENTS

PINEAPPLE &
TOASTED-COCONUT
SKEWERS • PAGE 79

PARSNIP CHIPS • PAGE 79

SPICED APPLE
WEDGES WITH
YOGURT • PAGE 79

FOREWORD

When we decided to create this book, the first question my editor asked was "How young is *too* young to cook?" I'm a firm believer in starting early. Include your children in food prep—even toddlers can measure flour, pick leaves from herbs, and wash berries. I'm not encouraging anyone to have a three-year-old chopping or frying, but building interest and comfort in the kitchen goes a long way in establishing culinary (and math) skills.

When I started to cook with my son, he'd wake up every Saturday morning and ask, "Mom, wanna cook with the machines?" This was my cue to get out the measuring cups and spoons and, of course, the mixer, blender, or food processor. He'd measure and dump dry ingredients, crack eggs (experience has taught us to do this into a smaller bowl—not straight into the batter . . .), and knead dough. By the time he went to kindergarten, we'd baked coffeecakes, scones, Dutch babies, pizzas, and more. And we'd also branched into cooking without machines.

This book provides young chefs with all the kitchen smarts they need. Tweens can test their wings by cooking our Triple-Decker Tortilla Pie (page 106), Crunchy Deviled Chicken (page 104), and Honey-Lime Ramen Salad (page 57) on their own. Or parents can follow our step-by-step guide to make Bunny Banana Pancakes (page 29) or a party-perfect Snake Cake (page 128) with younger children. *Kids Cook!* is full of easy, delicious recipes in a fun, accessible format. And true to our *Good Housekeeping* history, we include safety info, equipment musts, measuring tips, and eight important rules to follow before you begin. So . . . ready, set, cook! Here's to the next generation of confident cooks!

SUSAN WESTMORELAND
Food Director, *Good Housekeeping*

GET READY TO COOK!

Do you ever wish you could whip up a delicious dinner to impress your family or make a hearty breakfast to wow your friends after a sleepover? Then congratulations! You're holding *THE BOOK* for you! Whether it's creating to-die-for desserts, after-school snacks, or super-speedy lunches that will be the envy of the cafeteria, *Good Housekeeping Kids Cook!* has loads of dishes you'll love to make and love to eat. But first, take a few minutes to get familiar with these basics.

1. **READ** through the entire recipe.

2. **PREHEAT** the oven if the recipe says to do so. Set the timer for 15 minutes for the oven to reach the temperature you have set.

3. **WASH** your hands in warm, soapy water. Dry them thoroughly so they're not slippery.

4. **WEAR** an apron to protect your clothing and give you a place to quickly wipe your hands. If your shirt has long sleeves, roll them up. If your hair is long, tie it back.

5. **CLEAR** an area on the counter to cook. Wipe it down with a clean, damp sponge, then dry it thoroughly.

6. **CLEAN** fruits and veggies to remove any sand or grit. Give sturdy produce (like apples, carrots, and celery) a scrub with a soft-bristled brush, and then rinse and drain in a colander. Wash leafy greens and herbs in a salad spinner. Rinse berries in a colander and drain on paper towels.

7. **GATHER** all the utensils and ingredients listed in the recipe.

8. **MEASURE** out all the ingredients so that they are ready to use as soon as you start the recipe.

Knife Skills

You'll need a knife for practically every recipe in this book, so check with an adult to make sure it's sharp. (If a knife is dull, it's more likely to slip or get stuck in what you're cutting.) Use a wood or plastic cutting board every time you cut. This will protect the surface that you're working on and keep the blade of the knife from getting damaged. Here's how to use a knife properly and safely:

1. **CHOOSE** a knife that fits comfortably in your hand and doesn't feel too big.

2. **HOLD** the knife firmly by the handle. Make sure the sharp edge of the blade is facing down toward the food you are cutting. You can place your index finger over the top of the blade to help guide the knife.

3. **USE** your other hand to hold the food. Curl back your fingertips and thumb to keep them out of harm's way. Place the flat side of the food onto the cutting board. For round food (like a potato or an apple), you can cut a little slice off to give it a flat bottom. For a long ingredient (like a zucchini or carrot), cut it in half lengthwise first. This keeps the food from rolling away or slipping out of your hand.

4. **START** to cut by moving the knife away from your body. Focus on cutting and nothing else—accidents can happen if you're distracted.

Essential Knives

A **CHEF'S KNIFE** or French knife is an all-purpose knife used for slicing and chopping. A 5-inch knife is a good choice for kids.

A **SERRATED KNIFE** is long with "teeth" on the edge, which allows it to cut through baked goods like bread and cake.

A **PARING KNIFE** is shorter and used for trimming or peeling fruits and veggies.

Nutrition by Numbers

Food naturally contains nutrients—like protein, fat, and carbohydrates—that provide energy. Some nutrients, like fiber and sodium, don't provide energy but are also important for health. Your body needs the right combination of nutrients to work properly and grow. We've included the per-serving amount of each of these nutrients in every recipe so you know what you're eating.

Here are some terms to help you read nutritional information:

CALORIES tell you the total amount of energy in your food and can come from fat, protein, or carbohydrates. The amount of calories you need per day depends on your age, size, and activity level.

PROTEIN helps your body build and repair muscles, blood, and organs. High-protein foods include meat, poultry, fish, eggs, beans, lentils, nuts, and seeds.

FAT is an important nutrient that your body uses for growth and development. However, not all fats are the same. *Healthy fats* include vegetable and nut oils, which provide essential fatty acids and vitamin E. Healthy fat is also naturally found in avocados and seafood. On the other hand, *saturated fat*, which comes from animal sources like red meat, poultry, and full-fat dairy products, should be limited.

CARBOHYDRATES are your body's primary source of energy. You'll find *simple carbohydrates* in fruits, vegetables, and milk, as well as some sugars. *Complex carbohydrates* include whole-grain breads and cereals, starchy vegetables, and legumes (think beans and peanuts). Most complex carbs contain *fiber*, which makes you feel full and aids digestion.

Nutrients are weighed in grams (g) and milligrams (mg). One teaspoon of water weighs 5 grams; one teaspoon of sugar weighs about 4 grams.

SODIUM (translation: salt) is used by our bodies to conduct nerve impulses, contract and relax muscles, and stay hydrated—but you only need it in small amounts. Too much sodium in your diet can lead to high blood pressure, heart disease, and stroke.

Measure It Right

To ensure a recipe works, a cook needs to measure the ingredients accurately. Here are the essential tools and techniques you'll need:

A set of **metal or plastic measuring cups** includes ¼, ⅓, ½, and 1 cup measures.

FOR DRY AND SOLID INGREDIENTS
(LIKE FLOUR, SUGAR, BREAD CRUMBS, AND PEANUT BUTTER)

SPOON the ingredient into the correct-size metal or plastic measuring cup or spoon. Do not push down on the ingredient to pack it in (unless it's brown sugar, which should always be firmly packed when measured). Level off the top of the cup or spoon with the straight edge of a knife or spatula.

Graduated measuring spoons come as a set of ¼ teaspoon, ½ teaspoon, 1 teaspoon, and 1 tablespoon measures.

FOR WET INGREDIENTS
(LIKE BROTH, MILK, WATER, AND OIL)

PLACE the clear measuring cup on a flat surface. Pour the liquid into the cup until it reaches the desired line. Crouch down slightly so the measurement markings are at eye level. To measure a small amount of liquid, pour the liquid into a measuring spoon until it reaches the spoon's rim.

Clear measuring cups with spouts come in a 1-cup, 2-cup, 4-cup, and 8-cup capacity and are marked for measuring smaller amounts. No smaller markings? Use graduated measuring spoons.

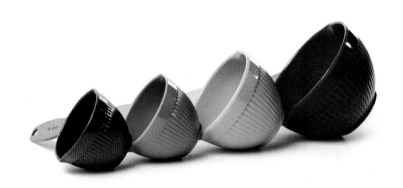

Cook's Lingo

Ready to start a recipe but not sure what a cooking term means? These simple definitions will help you as you go along!

BAKE To cook food in an oven, surrounded with dry heat; called "roasting" when applied to meat, poultry, or vegetables.

BEAT To stir quickly to make a mixture smooth using a whisk, spoon, fork, or mixer.

BLEND To thoroughly combine two or more ingredients, either by hand, with a whisk or spoon, or with a mixer.

BOIL To cook in hot, bubbling water that has reached 212°F.

BROIL To cook on a rack in an oven under direct heat.

CREAM To beat ingredients, usually sugar and a fat, like butter, until smooth and fluffy.

DICE To cut food into very small (1/8- to 1/4-inch) cubes.

GRATE To rub foods against a jagged surface to produce shredded or fine bits.

GRIND To reduce food to tiny pieces using a food processor.

PUREE To mash or grind food until completely smooth, usually in a food processor, blender, or sieve.

SHRED To cut food into small, thin strips with a knife or a grater.

SIMMER To cook in liquid just below the boiling point; bubbles should form but not burst on the surface of the liquid.

STIR-FRY To quickly cook small pieces of food over high heat, stirring constantly.

WHISK To beat ingredients (such as heavy cream, eggs, salad dressings, or sauces) with a fork or whisk in order to mix, blend, or add air.

Keep It Safe to Avoid Belly Aches

Raw meat, poultry, and seafood can contain germs (better known as bacteria) that can make you sick. So handle them carefully as follows:

- **PAT** any meat, poultry (chicken and turkey), or seafood you need in your recipe with paper towels, and then discard used towels. Place meat on a plate or tray and refrigerate until ready to use. Wash your hands afterward.

- **KEEP** meats and fish separate from other recipe ingredients. If a recipe calls for both raw meats and veggies, thoroughly wash knives, cutting boards, and utensils with hot soapy water when switching from meat to veggie preparation. Better yet, use separate cutting boards for meats and veggies.

- **STORE** all fresh food in the fridge until you are ready to use it.

- **TOSS** out any meat, poultry, or fish that looks discolored or smells bad.

- **NEVER** taste raw eggs, as they sometimes can contain bacteria, too.

- **THAW** frozen meat, poultry, or fish in the fridge overnight—not at room temperature.

- **KEEP** cold foods cold and hot foods hot. Perishable food should not be kept at room temperature for more than 2 hours. If you live somewhere warm, discard the food after 1 hour.

- **REFRIGERATE** or freeze any leftovers immediately after you've finished eating.

Now that you know the basics, are you ready to get started?

LET'S COOK!

1

Yummy Breakfasts

Do you have brekkie on the brain? That's good, because breakfast
is the most important meal of the day—especially for someone who's still growing.
Choose from foolproof eggs (plain or fancy), funny bunny pancakes,
true-blue berry muffins, and more (we've got brunch covered, too!). Your tummy
will thank you, and your day will no doubt be off to a strong start.

Classic
CHEESE OMELET

Eggs cook super quick. Be sure to have your seasonings
and cheese nearby and ready to go so you don't
accidentally overcook your omelet.

ACTIVE TIME → 15 MINUTES   TOTAL TIME → 20 MINUTES   MAKES → 4 SERVINGS

INGREDIENTS

8 large eggs

½ cup water

½ teaspoon salt

½ teaspoon coarsely
ground black pepper

2 tablespoons butter

4 ounces (½ cup)
shredded cheddar or
Swiss cheese

chopped green onions,
for garnish

toasted country-style
bread, optional

EACH SERVING

Calories: About 315
Protein: 20G
Carbohydrates: 2G
Total Fat: 25G
(Saturated Fat: 10G)
Fiber: 0G
Sodium: 670MG

1. Preheat oven to 200°F. Place 4 dinner plates in oven to warm. In medium bowl, place eggs, water, salt, and pepper. With fork, beat mixture with 25 to 30 quick strokes to blend without making it fluffy. (Overbeating toughens the proteins in the egg whites.)

2. In an 8-inch nonstick skillet, melt 1½ teaspoons butter over medium heat until hot. When butter stops sizzling, pour or ladle ½ cup egg mixture into skillet.

3. After egg mixture begins to set around edges (about 25 to 30 seconds), carefully push cooked egg from side of skillet toward center with heat-safe spatula so uncooked egg can reach bottom of hot skillet. Repeat 8 to 10 times around skillet, tilting as necessary, for 1 to 1½ minutes.

4. Cook until omelet is almost set but still creamy and moist on top. Place skillet handle facing you, and sprinkle ¼ cup cheese on half of omelet.

5. With spatula, fold uncovered half over filling.

6. Shake pan gently to loosen any egg or filling from edge, then slide omelet to edge of skillet. Holding skillet above warm plate, tip skillet so omelet slides onto plate. Keep warm in oven. Repeat with remaining butter, egg mixture, and cheese to make 4 omelets total. Sprinkle with green onions and serve with toast, if using.

Crustless
QUICHE LORRAINE

Pair this quiche with a green salad,
and you've got a quick and easy brunch.

ACTIVE TIME ➔ 15 MINUTES   TOTAL TIME ➔ 20 MINUTES   MAKES ➔ 4 SERVINGS

INGREDIENTS

6 large eggs

¼ cup whole milk

⅛ teaspoon salt

⅛ teaspoon ground black
pepper

4 ounces (½ cup)
shredded Gruyère
or Swiss cheese

1 teaspoon olive oil

3 slices thick-cut bacon,
chopped

1 medium shallot,
thinly sliced

snipped fresh chives,
optional

EACH SERVING

Calories: About 360
Protein: 22G
Carbohydrates: 3G
Total Fat: 29G
(Saturated Fat: 12G)
Fiber: 0G
Sodium: 555MG

1. Preheat oven to 375°F.

2. In large bowl with wire whisk, beat eggs, milk, salt, and pepper until combined; stir in cheese.

3. In 8-inch oven-safe nonstick skillet, heat oil over medium heat until hot. Add bacon and shallot. Cook for 6 minutes, or until bacon is crisp, stirring occasionally. Add eggs to skillet. Cook for 3 minutes, stirring occasionally, to form curds and allow runny egg to flow to bottom of pan.

4. Bake for 8 minutes or until top is set. Garnish with chives, if using.

HOW TO: WORK WITH EGGS

Before you whip up eggs, here are a few things you need to know:

SIZE Eggs are sold in different sizes. Our recipes call for large eggs, which are important for recipes like pancakes and baked items. If you're making scrambled or fried eggs, any size will do.

CRACKING Hold an egg in one hand. Gently but firmly tap the middle of the shell against the rim of a bowl until the shell cracks. Holding the egg over the bowl, pull the shell apart until the egg falls into the bowl.

SAFETY Start with chilled eggs (they should not sit out at room temperature more than 2 hours), and be sure to cook them until the whites are solid.

Bagel
BREAKFAST BAKE

We know you'll love everything about this bacon-egg-and-bagel casserole.
It's the perfect make-ahead dish for Sunday morning.

ACTIVE TIME → 10 MINUTES   TOTAL TIME → 1 HOUR 15 MINUTES (PLUS CHILLING AND COOLING)   MAKES → 6 SERVINGS

INGREDIENTS

4 "everything" bagels, toasted and chopped

6 large eggs

2 cups whole milk

4 ounces shredded Monterey Jack cheese (½ cup)

4 slices cooked bacon, finely chopped

4 green onions, sliced

½ teaspoon salt

¼ teaspoon ground black pepper

EACH SERVING

Calories: About 385
Protein: 21G
Carbohydrates: 39G
Total Fat: 16G
(Saturated Fat: 17G)
Fiber: 2G
Sodium: 805MG

1. Arrange bagels in 2- to 2½-quart baking dish.

2. In large bowl with wire whisk, beat eggs, milk, Monterey Jack, bacon, green onions, salt, and pepper. Pour over bagels, pressing down slightly to submerge. Cover and refrigerate for 1 hour or up to overnight.

3. Preheat oven to 350°F. Uncover dish and bake for 45 to 55 minutes or until center is set.

4. Cool for 15 minutes before serving.

HOW TO: COOK BACON

Grab a skillet and a pair of tongs, and follow these steps for crispy bacon every time.

1. ARRANGE sliced bacon in one layer in cold skillet.

2. SET the skillet over medium heat. When the bacon starts to crisp up and curl, loosen the slices with tongs.

3. TURN over each slice; cook, turning occasionally, until the bacon browns evenly.

4. DRAIN the bacon on paper towels. (If you're cooking lots of bacon, carefully pour the bacon fat into a small bowl after each batch.)

Mexican
BREAKFAST CHILAQUILES

This sizzling skillet scramble is like having nachos in the morning.

ACTIVE TIME → **15 MINUTES** **TOTAL TIME** → **20 MINUTES** (PLUS CHILLING AND COOLING) **MAKES** → **4 SERVINGS**

INGREDIENTS

6 large eggs

¼ teaspoon salt

1½ teaspoons vegetable oil

1 bag (5 ounces) tortilla chips

1 cup shredded Monterey Jack cheese

¼ cup pickled jalapeño slices

1 ripe avocado, thinly sliced

1 cup pico de gallo

2 tablespoons cilantro, chopped

sour cream and lime wedges, optional

EACH SERVING

Calories: About 360
Protein: 19G
Carbohydrates: 36G
Total Fat: 32G
(Saturated Fat: 9G)
Fiber: 6G
Sodium: 915MG

1. Preheat broiler. In large bowl with wire whisk, beat eggs and salt.

2. In oven-safe 12-inch nonstick skillet, heat oil over medium heat until hot. Add eggs and gently scramble for 3 to 4 minutes or until set. Transfer to bowl and set aside; wipe skillet mostly clean.

3. Spread half of chips in same skillet. Sprinkle with half of Monterey Jack. Top with remaining chips and cheese, then eggs and jalapeño.

4. Place skillet on broiling pan. Broil 6 inches from heat for 1 to 2 minutes or until cheese has melted and chips begin to brown.

5. Remove skillet from oven; top with avocado, pico de gallo, and cilantro. Serve with sour cream and lime wedges, if using.

SMART CHEF! Pickled jalapeño slices are spicy, so for a milder dish, use canned diced green chile peppers instead.

Green Eggs
& HAM'WICHES

Make the egg filling the night before, and throw together this gourmet grab-and-go breakfast sandwich in the morning. Or you can buy hard-cooked eggs from the salad bar at the supermarket and skip step 1.

ACTIVE TIME → 10 MINUTES   TOTAL TIME → 20 MINUTES (PLUS STANDING AND COOLING)   MAKES → 4 SERVINGS

INGREDIENTS

6 large eggs

¼ cup refrigerated basil pesto

3 tablespoons light mayonnaise

ground black pepper, to taste

4 croissants, halved

8 thin slices ham

1 cup arugula or baby spinach

EACH SERVING

Calories: About 500
Protein: 22G
Carbohydrates: 32G
Total Fat: 32G
(Saturated Fat: 11G)
Fiber: 2G
Sodium: 995MG

1. Place eggs in medium saucepan with enough cold water to cover by at least 1 inch. Heat just to boiling; remove pan from heat and cover. Let eggs stand for 15 minutes. Carefully pour out water; rinse eggs with cold running water to cool and stop the cooking. Gently tap each egg against hard surface until shell is cracked all over. Starting at the fatter rounded end, peel egg under cold running water. Allow the eggs to cool under the cold running water.

2. Chop eggs. In medium bowl, gently combine eggs, pesto, mayonnaise, and pepper.

3. Toast croissant halves. Divide ham, egg salad, and arugula among croissants. Serve immediately or wrap tightly in waxed paper and refrigerate for up to 4 hours.

SMART CHEF! Use a serrated knife with pointed or rounded teeth on the blade to split the croissants in half. That way the delicate pastry won't tear apart.

Bunny
BANANA PANCAKES

People will be hopping out of bed in the morning for a taste
of these adorable pancakes, and you only need three ingredients!
Very ripe bananas with brown peels are perfect for this recipe.

ACTIVE TIME → 15 MINUTES   **TOTAL TIME** → 30 MINUTES   **MAKES** → 4 SERVINGS

INGREDIENTS

2 very ripe large
bananas

3 large eggs

¾ cup self-rising flour

whipped cream,
sweetened flaked
coconut, banana slices,
and mini chocolate
chips for garnish,
optional

maple syrup,
optional

EACH SERVING

Calories: About 200
Protein: 8G
Carbohydrates: 33G
Total Fat: 4G
(Saturated Fat: 2G)
Fiber: 2G
Sodium: 335MG

1. Place large cookie sheet in oven and preheat to 225°F.

2. In blender, puree bananas until smooth. Add eggs; pulse until combined.
Pulse in flour until just combined.

3. Lightly grease griddle or 12-inch nonstick skillet; heat over medium heat
for 1 minute or until hot.

4. To make the bunny shapes, drop ¼ cup batter for body, 2 tablespoons
batter for head, 1 tablespoon batter in oval shape for each foot, and 1
tablespoon batter in elongated shape for each ear onto hot griddle. Cook
for 2 to 3 minutes or until bubbles start to form and edges look dry. With
spatula, turn pancakes, and cook for 1 to 2 minutes longer or until puffy
and underside is golden brown. Transfer pancakes to cookie sheet and
keep warm.

5. Repeat with remaining batter, greasing griddle again if necessary.
Arrange pancakes into bunny shapes on plates. Garnish with whipped
cream and coconut for tail and banana slices and chocolate chips for feet,
if using. Serve with maple syrup, if using.

The Ultimate
WAFFLES

Oats, chopped pecans, and a touch of cinnamon make these waffles extra special.

ACTIVE TIME → **10 MINUTES**   **TOTAL TIME** → **30 MINUTES** (PLUS SOAKING)   **MAKES** → **8 SERVINGS**

INGREDIENTS

½ cup old-fashioned oats, uncooked

1½ cups low-fat buttermilk

1 cup whole wheat flour

1 cup pecans, chopped

2 teaspoons baking powder

½ teaspoon baking soda

½ teaspoon cinnamon

½ teaspoon salt

2 large eggs

3 tablespoons vegetable oil

2 tablespoons honey

1 tablespoon vanilla extract

2 cups strawberries

butter and honey for serving, optional

EACH SERVING

Calories: About 295
Protein: 8G
Carbohydrates: 25G
Total Fat: 19G
(Saturated Fat: 2G)
Fiber: 4G
Sodium: 430MG

1. Preheat oven to 225°F.

2. In medium bowl, combine oats and buttermilk. Let soak for 20 minutes.

3. Preheat waffle maker. In large bowl with wire whisk, mix flour, pecans, baking powder, baking soda, cinnamon, and salt. In medium bowl, whisk eggs, oil, honey, and vanilla until blended. Add egg mixture and oat mixture to flour mixture. Stir until just combined (small lumps are okay).

4. Spray waffle maker with nonstick cooking spray. Pour ⅓ cup batter onto heated waffle maker. Close waffle maker; cook for 3 minutes or until deep golden brown. Place waffle directly on oven rack to keep warm. Repeat with remaining batter.

5. Serve with strawberries, butter, and more honey, if using.

SMART CHEF! Freeze half the waffles for another almost-instant breakfast! Cool at room temperature, then wrap individual waffles in plastic and store in resealable plastic bags in the freezer for up to 1 month. Reheat in toaster oven, or a 350°F oven, for 8 to 10 minutes.

Smoothie Bowl
THREE WAYS

Here are three smoothies you can eat with a spoon, each loaded with toppings—sundae-style! We piled the Tropical Smoothie Bowl (below) with chopped almonds, shredded coconut, fresh kiwi, mango, and blueberries. Not your style? Add your own toppings! Use whatever is crunchy or fresh. All recipes serve 2.

Tropical Smoothie Bowl

In blender, pulse **1 ripe banana**, sliced and frozen; **1 cup frozen mango chunks**; **1 cup frozen pineapple chunks**; and **1 cup almond milk** until mixture is smooth but still thick. Stop the blender and stir occasionally. Add more liquid if needed. Pour into 2 bowls. Top as desired.

EACH SERVING: About 180 Calories, 3G Protein, 43G Carbohydrates, 2G Total Fat (0G Saturated), 5G Fiber, 90MG Sodium

Berry-Coconut Smoothie Bowl

In blender, pulse **1 ripe banana**, sliced and frozen; **2 cups frozen mixed berries**; and **1 cup coconut water** until mixture is smooth but still thick, stopping and stirring occasionally. Add more liquid if needed. Pour into 2 bowls. Top as desired.

EACH SERVING: About 160 Calories, 2G Protein, 39G Carbohydrates, 1G Total Fat (0G Saturated), 7G Fiber, 20MG Sodium

Orange-Peach Smoothie Bowl

In blender, pulse **1 ripe banana**, sliced and frozen; **1½ cups frozen peaches**; **½ cup nonfat Greek yogurt**; and **¾ cup orange juice** until mixture is smooth but still thick, stopping and stirring occasionally. Add more liquid if needed. Pour into 2 bowls. Top as desired.

EACH SERVING: About 195 Calories, 13G Protein, 45G Carbohydrates, 0G Total Fat (0G Saturated), 3G Fiber, 28MG Sodium

Peach Melba
BREAKFAST POPS

Looking for a cool breakfast for a hot summer day? These creamy, crunchy, no-spoon-required pops are the perfect treat.

ACTIVE TIME → 10 MINUTES   TOTAL TIME → 6 TO 8 HOURS (WITH FREEZING)   MAKES → 6 SERVINGS

INGREDIENTS

⅔ cup vanilla Greek yogurt

2 tablespoons honey

2 small ripe peaches, chopped (about 1½ cups)

¼ cup raspberries, halved

½ cup granola

EACH SERVING

Calories: About 95
Protein: 3G
Carbohydrates: 30G
Total Fat: 1G
(Saturated Fat: 1G)
Fiber: 2G
Sodium: 30MG

1. In blender, combine yogurt, honey, and three-fourths of peaches until mixture is smooth.

2. Distribute raspberries and remaining peaches among 6 to 8 ice pop molds. Fill each mold with about ¼ cup yogurt mixture, tapping to distribute, leaving ½ inch unfilled. Top with granola; pack granola tightly into yogurt until yogurt reaches top of mold.

3. Freeze for 6 to 8 hours or until solid.

Whole-Grain
BLUEBERRY MUFFINS

Everybody loves blueberry muffins, especially when they're topped with crunchy almond sugar.

ACTIVE TIME → **20 MINUTES**   **TOTAL TIME** → **40 MINUTES** (PLUS COOLING)   **MAKES** → **12 MUFFINS**

INGREDIENTS

1 cup old-fashioned oats, uncooked

1 cup whole wheat flour

½ cup all-purpose flour

¼ cup plus 1 tablespoon packed brown sugar

2 teaspoons baking powder

½ teaspoon baking soda

½ teaspoon salt

1 cup low-fat buttermilk

¼ cup orange juice

2 tablespoons vegetable oil

1 large egg

1 teaspoon vanilla extract

2 cups blueberries

EACH MUFFIN

Calories: About 170
Protein: 5G
Carbohydrates: 28G
Total Fat: 5G
(Saturated Fat: 1G)
Fiber: 3G
Sodium: 270MG

1. Preheat oven to 400°F. Line 12-cup muffin pan with paper liners.

2. In blender, place oats and blend until finely ground. In large bowl with wire whisk, mix oats, whole wheat flour, all-purpose flour, ¼ cup sugar, baking powder, baking soda, and salt. In small bowl with wire whisk, mix buttermilk, juice, oil, egg, and vanilla until blended. With rubber spatula, fold egg mixture into flour mixture until combined; fold in blueberries.

3. Combine nuts and remaining 1 tablespoon sugar. Divide batter among prepared muffin cups; sprinkle with almond sugar. Bake for 22 minutes or until toothpick inserted in centers of muffins comes out clean. Cool in pan on wire rack for 5 minutes. Remove muffins from pan; cool completely on wire rack.

HOW TO: FOLD INGREDIENTS

"Fold" means to mix in such a way that light ingredients, like eggs and liquids, are evenly distributed throughout a heavier ingredient, such as flour, without overmixing a batter. Here's the technique:

PLACE the lighter mixture on top of the heavier mixture in a bowl.

STARTING from one side, cut down the center of the mixtures with a spatula.

SCRAPE the spatula along the bottom of the bowl and up the other side, gently lifting the bottom mixture and turning it over the top mixture.

TURN the bowl a quarter turn and repeat steps 1 through 3 until everything is just combined. (If small streaks of dry ingredients remain, that's okay.)

Spiced Banana-Chocolate
MUFFINS

Get ready to splurge for breakfast this morning!

ACTIVE TIME → 15 MINUTES   TOTAL TIME → 35 MINUTES (PLUS COOLING)   MAKES → 18 MUFFINS

INGREDIENTS

2 cups old-fashioned oats, uncooked

1¼ cups white whole wheat flour

½ cup packed brown sugar

2 teaspoons baking powder

¾ teaspoon baking soda

½ teaspoon salt

½ teaspoon ground cinnamon

¼ teaspoon ground ginger

1¼ cups mashed banana

1 cup low-fat buttermilk

2 tablespoons vegetable oil

1 large egg, beaten

2 ounces bittersweet chocolate, melted

EACH MUFFIN

Calories: About 140
Protein: 3G
Carbohydrates: 23G
Total Fat: 4G
(Saturated Fat: 1G)
Fiber: 1G
Sodium: 198MG

1. Preheat oven to 400°F. Line 18 muffin-pan cups with paper liners.

2. In large bowl with wire whisk, mix oats, flour, sugar, baking powder, baking soda, salt, cinnamon, and ginger. In medium bowl, whisk bananas, buttermilk, oil, and egg until blended. With rubber spatula, fold banana mixture into flour mixture until just combined. Divide batter among prepared muffin cups.

3. Bake for 20 to 25 minutes or until toothpick inserted in centers of muffins comes out clean. Cool in pans on wire racks for 10 minutes. Remove muffins from pans; cool completely on wire racks.

4. Drizzle tops with chocolate.

SMART CHEF! No buttermilk? Make your own: Put 1 tablespoon white vinegar or lemon juice in a 1-cup liquid measuring cup. Fill the cup with milk to the 1-cup line and stir with a spoon.

Carrot Muffin
BABY BUNDTS

Here's a sweet surprise for brunch or for a special brekkie in bed for your parents.

ACTIVE TIME → 20 MINUTES   **TOTAL TIME** → 35 MINUTES (PLUS COOLING)   **MAKES** → 6 SERVINGS

INGREDIENTS

1½ cups white whole wheat flour

1½ cups grated carrots

½ cup packed brown sugar

1 teaspoon baking soda

1½ teaspoons pumpkin pie spice

¼ teaspoon salt

2 large eggs

⅓ cup applesauce

¼ cup vegetable oil

1 teaspoon vanilla extract

2 ounces cream cheese, softened

3 tablespoon confectioners' sugar

2 to 3 tablespoons whole milk

EACH SERVING WITH GLAZE

Calories: About 345
Protein: 7G
Carbohydrates: 44G
Total Fat: 15G
(Saturated Fat: 3G)
Fiber: 4G
Sodium: 370MG

1. Preheat oven to 375°F. Coat 6 cups of mini Bundt pan with nonstick cooking spray.

2. In large bowl, combine flour, carrots, brown sugar, baking soda, pie spice, and ¼ teaspoon salt. In medium bowl with wire whisk, beat eggs, applesauce, oil, and vanilla. With rubber spatula, stir egg mixture into flour mixture just until blended; divide among Bundt pan cups.

3. Bake for 14 to 16 minutes or until toothpick inserted into centers of cakes comes out clean. Cool in pan on wire rack for 5 minutes. Transfer cakes from pan to rack to cool completely.

4. Meanwhile, beat cream cheese, confectioners' sugar, and milk until smooth and slightly runny. Drizzle cooled cakes with glaze.

SMART CHEF! If you don't have white whole wheat flour, substitute 1½ cups all-purpose flour or ¾ cup each all-purpose flour and whole wheat flour.

Grab 'N' Go
CRANBERRY GRANOLA BARS

Next time you bake, have some delicious fun with the most important meal of the day.

ACTIVE TIME → **15 MINUTES**   **TOTAL TIME** → **45 MINUTES** (PLUS COOLING)   **MAKES** → **16 SERVINGS**

INGREDIENTS

2 cups old-fashioned oats, uncooked

½ cup honey

½ cup vegetable oil

2 large egg whites

2 tablespoons packed brown sugar

1 teaspoon ground cinnamon

½ teaspoon salt

¾ cup toasted wheat germ

¾ cup chopped walnuts

¾ cup dried cranberries

EACH SERVING

Calories: About 215
Protein: 5G
Carbohydrates: 25G
Total Fat: 12G
(Saturated Fat: 1G)
Fiber: 3G
Sodium: 80MG

1. Preheat oven to 325°F. Line 13-by-9-inch baking pan with foil, leaving 2-inch overhang; spray foil with nonstick cooking spray.

2. Spread oats on large microwave-safe plate. Microwave on High in 1-minute intervals for 4 to 5 minutes or until fragrant and golden, stirring between intervals. Cool.

3. In large bowl with wire whisk, mix honey, oil, 2 tablespoons water, egg whites, sugar, cinnamon, and salt until well blended. With rubber spatula, fold oats, wheat germ, walnuts, and dried cranberries into honey mixture until blended; transfer to prepared pan. Using wet hands, press dough into even layer. Bake for 28 to 30 minutes or until golden. Cool in pan on wire rack.

4. Using foil, transfer to cutting board; cut into 16 bars. Store in airtight container at room temperature for up to 4 days, or freeze for up to 1 month.

SMART CHEF! A microwave-safe plate is made of glass or ceramic and is marked "heatproof" or "microwave-safe." Make sure to use oven mitts when removing the plate from the oven to protect yourself from the heat.

2

Lunches to Go

Bye-bye, boring brown-bag lunch—hello, delicious! We know it's hectic getting ready for school, so we've done the homework for you. Each recipe (including piping-hot soups and chili, zesty salads, hearty sandwich wraps, and more) is either do-ahead easy, ready in a flash—or both! Most recipes make four lunches—enough for leftovers or to share with the family. Are you ready for some seriously fun food prep? Let's get started!

Veggie Wraps
WITH GOAT CHEESE

This hearty sandwich is chock-full of mushrooms, red pepper, and green beans
(and we roast the veggies so they taste extra sweet).

ACTIVE TIME → **15 MINUTES**   **TOTAL TIME** → **45 MINUTES**   **MAKES** → **4 SERVINGS**

INGREDIENTS

2 portobello mushroom
caps, sliced

1 large red pepper, sliced

8 ounces green beans,
trimmed

2 tablespoons olive oil

¼ teaspoon salt

2 cans (15 ounces each)
chickpeas, rinsed and
drained

3 tablespoons fresh
lemon juice

¼ teaspoon ground
black pepper

1 ounce goat cheese,
crumbled

4 soft taco-size whole-
grain tortillas

lemon wedges

EACH SERVING

Calories: About 465
Protein: 19G
Carbohydrates: 66G
Total Fat: 16G
(Saturated Fat: 3G)
Fiber: 17G
Sodium: 910MG

1. Arrange oven racks in top and bottom third of oven. Preheat oven to
450°F.

2. In large bowl, combine mushrooms, red pepper, green beans, oil, and salt,
tossing to coat. Divide between 2 large rimmed baking sheets, spreading
vegetables in even layer. Roast 30 minutes or until vegetables are tender.

3. Meanwhile, in large bowl, mash chickpeas, lemon juice and pepper; spread
evenly on tortillas.

4. Top tortillas evenly with vegetables and goat cheese. Fold to wrap. Serve
with lemon wedges.

SMART CHEF! Roast the veggies and make the chickpea mixture a
day ahead; transfer to airtight containers and refrigerate. All that's
left for the next day is to crumble the cheese and assemble the
sandwiches.

45

FUN FOOD!

Best Chicken
SALAD

Plain or fancy, chicken salad is always a treat. Here's our basic recipe plus three tasty twists that make it extra special.

TOTAL TIME → 15 MINUTES   MAKES → 4 SERVINGS

INGREDIENTS

3 stalks celery, finely chopped

¼ cup mayonnaise

2 teaspoons fresh lemon juice

¼ teaspoon salt

¼ teaspoon ground black pepper

3 cups rotisserie chicken breast meat, cut into bite-size pieces

EACH SERVING

Calories: About 240
Protein: 30G
Carbohydrates: 1G
Total Fat: 13G
(Saturated Fat: 2G)
Fiber: 0G
Sodium: 592MG

1. In medium bowl, combine celery, mayonnaise, lemon juice, salt, and pepper; stir until blended. Add chicken and toss to coat.

Basil-Sundried Tomato

Prepare recipe as directed, but add ¼ cup chopped fresh basil and 2 tablespoons finely chopped, oil-packed, sun-dried tomatoes, drained, to mayonnaise mixture.

EACH SERVING: About 250 Calories, 30G Protein, 2G Carbohydrate, 13G Total Fat (2G Saturated), 0G Fiber, 601MG Sodium

Curry-Grape

Prepare recipe as directed, but add 2 cups red or green seedless grapes, cut in half, 1 teaspoon curry powder, and 1 teaspoon honey to mayonnaise mixture.

EACH SERVING: About 300 Calories, 30G Protein, 16G Carbohydrate, 13G Total Fat (2G Saturated), 1G Fiber, 593MG Sodium

Lemon-Pepper

Prepare recipe as directed, but use 1 tablespoon fresh lemon juice and ½ teaspoon coarsely ground black pepper; add ½ teaspoon freshly grated lemon peel.

EACH SERVING: About 240 Calories, 30G Protein, 1G Carbohydrate, 13G Total Fat (2G Saturated), 0G Fiber, 592MG Sodium

Tuna
SALAD

Veggies add flavor and crunch to this lunchtime staple. We love it on ciabatta bread.

TOTAL TIME → 15 MINUTES   MAKES → 4 SERVINGS

INGREDIENTS

2 cans (5 ounces each) chunk light tuna in water, drained

2 medium stalks celery, chopped

1 medium carrot, shredded

½ medium red pepper, chopped

¼ cup light mayonnaise

3 tablespoons nonfat plain yogurt

1 tablespoon fresh lemon juice

¼ teaspoon ground black pepper

EACH SERVING WITHOUT BREAD

Calories: About 135
Protein: 16G
Carbohydrates: 6G
Total Fat: 6G
(Saturated Fat: 1G)
Fiber: 1G
Sodium: 340MG

1. In medium bowl, combine tuna, celery, carrot, red pepper, mayonnaise, yogurt, lemon juice, and black pepper.

HOW TO: PACK A SAFE LUNCH

Bacteria that cause food poisoning can grow at room temperature in just two hours. To make sure your lunch is safe and properly packed, follow these rules:

PREPARE cooked food ahead of time to allow for thorough chilling in the refrigerator. Divide food into shallow containers for fast chilling. If you made lunch the night before, don't put it in your backpack until you're ready to leave home.

PACK just the amount of perishable food you're going to eat. That way the storage or safety of leftovers won't be a problem. After lunch, discard all leftover food, used disposable food packaging, and paper bags.

USE an insulated container (like a thermos) to keep hot food hot. Fill the container with boiling water and let stand for a few minutes. Empty it and then put in the piping-hot food. Keep the container closed until lunchtime.

CHOOSE insulated lunch boxes or bags to keep food cold, and pack frozen gel packs or combine a frozen gel pack with a frozen juice box or frozen bottle of water. Place gel packs on the top and bottom of the perishable food.

Turkey & Cucumber
SALAD WRAPS

You'll find a double dose of fruit in every bite.

TOTAL TIME → 30 MINUTES   MAKES → 4 SERVINGS

INGREDIENTS

¼ cup mayonnaise

¼ cup mango chutney

ground black pepper

2 cups chopped cantaloupe (about ½ medium cantaloupe)

½ small English (seedless) cucumber, chopped

½ cup packed fresh cilantro leaves

4 burrito-size flour tortillas

2 cups mixed greens

1 pound thinly sliced reduced-sodium deli-smoked turkey

EACH SERVING

Calories: About 570
Protein: 37G
Carbohydrates: 60G
Total Fat: 22G
(Saturated Fat: 6G)
Fiber: 3G
Sodium: 1,540MG

1. In large bowl, combine mayonnaise, chutney, and pepper. Add cantaloupe, cucumber, and cilantro, tossing to combine.

2. Working with 1 tortilla at a time, place about ¾ cup cantaloupe mixture, ½ cup greens, and ¼ pound turkey in center of tortilla. Fold in sides and roll tightly around filling. Serve immediately, or wrap tightly in foil or plastic wrap and refrigerate for up to 3 hours.

HOW TO: CREATE A COMBO!

Looking for lunch ideas that will excite your appetite? Whether it's a picnic, school trip, or tailgate lunch, we've got three terrific menus to fit the bill (plus dessert!).

MENU ONE Tomato Soup with Cupid Croutons (page 63) + **Lemon-Pepper Chicken Salad** (page 47) + Crispy Chocolate-Chip Cookies (page 133)

MENU TWO Broccoli Soup (page 60) + **Veggie Wraps with Goat Cheese** (page 45) + **Home-Style Banana Bread** (page 143)

MENU THREE Tex-Mex Chicken Soup (page 59) + **Burrito "Bowl"** (page 55) + **Watermelon Pizza** (page 147)

Veggie
FOCACCIA

This fancy sandwich is a snap to put together!

TOTAL TIME → 20 MINUTES   MAKES → 4 SERVINGS

INGREDIENTS

1 tablespoon red wine vinegar

1 tablespoon extra virgin olive oil

1 small shallot, finely chopped

½ teaspoon fresh thyme leaves, chopped

⅛ teaspoon salt

⅛ teaspoon freshly ground black pepper

1 jar (9 to 10 ounces) artichoke hearts, rinsed, drained, and cut into quarters

1 jar (16 ounces) roasted red peppers, patted dry

3 ounces baby spinach leaves (5 cups)

4 (5-inch-square) pieces focaccia bread

¼ cup prepared basil pesto

2 tablespoons mayonnaise

1 pound (1 large ball) fresh mozzarella cheese, thinly sliced

1. In small bowl with wire whisk, mix vinegar, oil, shallot, thyme, salt, and pepper until blended. Place artichokes in a medium bowl, peppers in another bowl, and spinach in a third bowl. Divide dressing among all 3 bowls. Toss all food in bowls until well coated.

2. With serrated knife, split each focaccia square horizontally in half. In another small bowl, mix pesto and mayonnaise. Spread on all cut sides of focaccia.

3. On each bottom half of focaccia, layer one-fourth each of spinach, peppers, mozzarella, and artichokes. Replace top halves of focaccia.

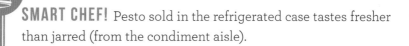

SMART CHEF! Pesto sold in the refrigerated case tastes fresher than jarred (from the condiment aisle).

EACH SERVING

Calories: About 785
Protein: 31G
Carbohydrates: 69G
Total Fat: 43G
(Saturated Fat: 18G)
Fiber: 4G
Sodium: 1,260MG

FUN FOOD!

Salads IN A JAR

These prep-ahead lunch salads will help you make the most of last night's meal. In a mason jar, pour in the dressing first, then add leftover grains, protein (e.g., beans, chicken, tuna), and sturdy veggies. Top with delicate foods like lettuce and cheese. Pop on the lid and set in your lunch bag. Ready to eat? Just grab a fork and dig in! All recipes serve 1.

Burrito "Bowl"

In 16-ounce mason jar, layer 2 tablespoons Southwestern ranch dressing;
¼ cup canned black beans, rinsed and drained; ¼ cup corn kernels;
¼ avocado, chopped; ⅓ cup cooked rice; 1 cup chopped romaine lettuce;
and 1 tablespoon shredded cheddar cheese.

EACH SERVING: About 395 Calories, 9G Protein, 39G Carbohydrate, 23G Total Fat
(4G Saturated), 8G Fiber, 497MG Sodium

Sesame Chicken Slaw

In 16-ounce mason jar, layer 2 tablespoons sesame-ginger dressing,
½ cup chopped red cabbage, ½ cup chopped cooked chicken, ¼ cup
shredded carrots, ½ cup cooked quinoa, and 2 tablespoons
dry-roasted edamame or wasabi peas.

EACH SERVING: About 410 Calories, 29G Protein, 35G Carbohydrate, 16G Total Fat
(3G Saturated), 7G Fiber, 402MG Sodium

Pasta Salad

In 16-ounce mason jar, layer 2 tablespoons balsamic vinaigrette;
½ cup cooked pasta; ¼ cup chopped cucumbers; 5 grape tomatoes, halved;
¼ cup canned cannellini beans, rinsed and drained; ½ cup baby spinach;
and fresh basil leaves.

EACH SERVING: About 255 Calories, 9G Protein, 39G Carbohydrate, 5G Total Fat
(0G Saturated), 1G Fiber, 452MG Sodium

Honey-Lime
RAMEN SALAD

This recipe will remind you of cold sesame noodles, only with a fresher taste.

ACTIVE TIME → 20 MINUTES   **TOTAL TIME →** 30 MINUTES   **MAKES →** 4 SERVINGS

INGREDIENTS

8 ounces Chinese curly egg noodles (or ramen noodles)

¼ cup tahini (sesame seed paste)

3 tablespoons soy sauce

3 tablespoons fresh lime juice

1 tablespoon honey

2 garlic cloves, crushed with press

1 large English (seedless) cucumber, chopped

1 pint grape tomatoes, halved

3 cups thinly sliced Napa or savoy cabbage

¼ cup finely chopped fresh cilantro

EACH SERVING

Calories: About 360
Protein: 14G
Carbohydrates: 56G
Total Fat: 10G
(Saturated Fat: 2G)
Fiber: 6G
Sodium: 680MG

1. Cook noodles as label directs.

2. Meanwhile, in large bowl with wire whisk, mix tahini, soy sauce, lime juice, honey, and garlic until smooth. Add cucumber, tomatoes, and cabbage, tossing until well coated.

3. Drain noodles and rinse with cold water. Drain once more, shaking off as much excess water as possible. Add to bowl with vegetables along with cilantro. Toss until well combined. Serve immediately or refrigerate, covered, up to 1 day.

?

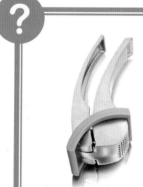

WHAT IS IT?

A **GARLIC PRESS** is a tool used for crushing garlic cloves through small holes to extract the pulp, oils, and juice. (Very handy when you don't feel like chopping.) The garlic pulp remaining on the press dries quickly, so it's best to clean the press immediately after using.

Tex-Mex
CHICKEN SOUP

This hearty soup is comfort on a chilly day! If you want it less spicy,
reduce the chili powder to 1 teaspoon.

ACTIVE TIME → 15 MINUTES   TOTAL TIME → 30 MINUTES   MAKES → 4 SERVINGS

INGREDIENTS

2 tablespoons
vegetable oil

1 large onion, finely
chopped

1½ teaspoons chili
powder

1 carton (32 ounces) lower-
sodium chicken broth

12 ounces rotisserie
chicken breast
meat, shredded
(about 2¾ cups)

2 cups frozen
(thawed) corn

2 tablespoons fresh
lime juice

2 tablespoons finely
chopped fresh cilantro

1 ripe avocado, chopped,
for garnish

EACH SERVING

Calories: About 385
Protein: 33G
Carbohydrates: 25G
Total Fat: 20G
(Saturated Fat: 3G)
Fiber: 6G
Sodium: 410MG

1. In 5-quart saucepot, heat oil over medium-high heat until hot. Add onion
and chili powder; cook for 5 minutes or until onion starts to brown, stirring.

2. Add chicken broth; heat to just to simmering over high heat. Stir in
chicken, corn, lime juice, and cilantro. Reduce heat to medium and simmer
for 5 minutes or until flavors are blended. Divide soup among 4 serving
bowls. Garnish with avocado.

HOW TO: CHOOSE A RIPE AVOCADO

There are many different types of avocados, but Hass avocados, which have
dark-green, bumpy skin and rich, creamy insides, are our pick for recipes.
Like other fruits (bananas, for example), avocados need to be ripe before
they're ready to use. Follow these steps when checking for ripeness:

1. Place an avocado in the palm of your hand.

2. Gently squeeze without applying your fingertips (this can cause bruising).

3. If the avocado feels tender (but not mushy), it's ripe and ready to eat. If
the avocado feels firm, give it a couple of days before checking again.

Broccoli
SOUP

Got leftover mashed potatoes (like our Super-Creamy Potatoes, page 124)?
Make soup! This recipe is extra cheesy.

ACTIVE TIME → 10 MINUTES   TOTAL TIME → 25 MINUTES   MAKES → 4 SERVINGS

INGREDIENTS

1 carton (32 ounces)
lower-sodium
chicken broth

1 package (10 ounces)
frozen broccoli florets,
thawed

2 cups leftover mashed
potatoes

⅛ teaspoon ground
black pepper

8 ounces (1 cup)
shredded cheddar cheese

lemon slices, chopped
parsley, and shredded
cheddar cheese, optional

EACH SERVING

Calories: About 370
Protein: 16G
Carbohydrates: 24G
Total Fat: 22G
(Saturated Fat: 11G)
Fiber: 3G
Sodium: 1,158MG

1. In blender, puree broth and broccoli until smooth. Transfer to 4-quart saucepot. Heat to boiling over medium-high heat. With wire whisk, stir in potatoes and pepper until blended.

2. Reduce heat to low. Simmer 10 minutes. Stir in cheddar until melted and smooth. Top with lemon slices, parsley, and more cheddar, if using.

Turkey
& WHITE BEAN CHILI

Nothing beats chili for a hot lunch. And this recipe is so versatile—you can swap in lean ground beef for the turkey, or red kidney or black beans for the white beans.

ACTIVE TIME → **15 MINUTES**   **TOTAL TIME** → **35 MINUTES**   **MAKES** → **4 SERVINGS**

INGREDIENTS

1 tablespoon olive oil

1 pound lean (93%) ground turkey

½ teaspoon salt

1 medium onion, chopped

4 teaspoons chili powder

1 tablespoon ground cumin

1 can (28 ounces) whole tomatoes in juice, chopped

1 can (15 to 19 ounces) white kidney beans (cannellini), rinsed and drained

½ cup plain nonfat yogurt

EACH SERVING

Calories: About 380
Protein: 33G
Carbohydrates: 35G
Total Fat: 13G
(Saturated Fat: 3G)
Fiber: 10G
Sodium: 875MG

1. In 12-inch skillet, heat oil over medium-high heat until hot. Add turkey and salt. Cook, stirring and breaking up turkey with side of spoon, for 6 to 8 minutes or until turkey loses its pink color throughout.

2. Add onion and cook for 4 minutes or until tender. Stir in chili powder and cumin; cook for 1 minute.

3. Add tomatoes with their juice, beans, and ½ cup water; heat to boiling over high heat. Reduce heat to medium and cook, uncovered, for 10 minutes or until flavors are blended, stirring occasionally. Ladle chili among 4 serving bowls and top with a dollop of yogurt.

Tomato Soup
WITH CUPID CROUTONS

Ladle up a little love. Our tomato soup is super-filling and loaded with vitamin C.
Not to mention, the heart-shaped croutons are sure to win everyone's affection!

ACTIVE TIME → **15 MINUTES**   **TOTAL TIME** → **45 MINUTES**   **MAKES** → **4 SERVINGS**

INGREDIENTS

2 tablespoons olive oil

1 medium onion, chopped

2 garlic cloves, chopped

3 cups lower-sodium vegetable or chicken broth

1 can (28 ounces) whole peeled tomatoes

2 bay leaves

½ teaspoon salt

4 slices white bread

1 tablespoon butter

½ teaspoon sugar

¼ teaspoon ground black pepper

EACH SERVING

Calories: About 220
Protein: 4G
Carbohydrates: 27G
Total Fat: 11G
(Saturated Fat: 3G)
Fiber: 3G
Sodium: 928MG

1. In 5- to 6-quart saucepot, heat oil over medium heat until hot. Add onion and garlic; cook for 10 minutes or until tender, stirring. Add broth, tomatoes, bay leaves, and ½ teaspoon salt; heat to boiling over high heat. Reduce heat; simmer for 20 minutes, stirring occasionally.

2. Prepare heart croutons: Meanwhile, trim crusts from bread. With small, heart-shaped cookie cutter, cut hearts from bread slices; toast hearts in a toaster oven or by broiling on a sheet pan in the oven for a few minutes, until golden brown in color. Stir bread scraps into soup.

3. Remove and discard bay leaves. Stir in butter and sugar. In blender at low speed, with center part of blender's lid removed to allow steam to escape, blend tomato mixture in batches until smooth. Pour soup into large bowl after each batch. Return soup to same saucepan; stir in pepper. Heat through. Divide soup among 4 mugs. Serve topped with croutons.

SMART CHEF! Never fill a blender more than half full with hot liquid. When you turn the blender on, it can overflow and burn you (or the built-up steam can blow the lid off the blender). To be safe, let the mixture cool for a few minutes before you start. Blend in small batches at the lowest speed with the center part of the lid removed so that steam can escape.

3

Super Snacks & Sips

Whether you're craving chips, dips, or tasty bites . . . hot cocoa, lemonade, or sparkling punch. . . . Whether it's sweet, savory, crunchy, or creamy, we've got you covered! The next time a craving calls, try one of these satisfying options.

Pretzel
BITES

Pretzels are a traditional treat, and this recipe is packed with flavor! Try these and you won't be going back to pretzels from the vending machine any time soon.

ACTIVE TIME → 20 MINUTES   TOTAL TIME → 40 MINUTES   MAKES → 3 DOZEN BITES

INGREDIENTS

1¼ pounds fresh or frozen (thawed) pizza dough, at room temperature

⅓ cup baking soda

1 large egg, beaten

coarse sea salt

Dijon mustard with seeds, for serving

EACH BITE

Calories: About 35
Protein: 1G
Carbohydrates: 6G
Total Fat: 0G
(Saturated Fat: 0G)
Fiber: 0G
Sodium: 507MG

1. Preheat oven to 450°F. Line 1 large rimmed baking sheet with double layer of paper towels and 2 large cookie sheets with parchment paper.

2. Roll pizza dough into 36 cherry-size balls (about ½ ounce each).

3. In small pot, bring 5 cups water to boiling over high heat. Stir in baking soda.

4. Working in batches, drop balls into boiling water. Boil for 1 minute or until slightly puffed. With slotted spoon, remove balls and place on paper towels; drain. Place balls ½ inch apart on prepared cooking sheet. Brush with egg; sprinkle with salt.

5. Bake for 12 to 15 minutes or until golden. Serve with mustard.

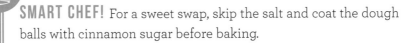

SMART CHEF! For a sweet swap, skip the salt and coat the dough balls with cinnamon sugar before baking.

Cocoa
CROISSANTS

Transform store-bought ingredients into fancy pastry shop treats!

ACTIVE TIME → 15 MINUTES   TOTAL TIME → 40 MINUTES   MAKES → 8 SERVINGS

INGREDIENTS

1 sheet frozen (thawed) puff pastry

16 teaspoons chocolate-hazelnut spread

1 large egg, beaten

EACH SERVING

Calories: About 200
Protein: 3G
Carbohydrates: 17G
Total Fat: 12G
(Saturated Fat: 3G)
Fiber: 0G
Sodium: 163MG

1. Preheat oven to 400°F. Line 1 large cookie sheet with parchment paper.

2. On lightly floured surface, roll pastry into 14-inch square. Cut pastry into quarters to form 4 squares. Cut each square diagonally to form 8 triangles.

3. Spread 2 teaspoons chocolate-hazelnut spread on each triangle; starting at wider end, roll up pastry. Place rolls on parchment-lined cookie sheet. Lightly brush rolls with egg.

4. Bake for 23 to 25 minutes or until pastry is golden brown.

SMART CHEF! Allow frozen puff pastry to thaw for 45 minutes at room temperature, or overnight in the fridge. Gently unfold the thawed pastry before rolling. If you see any tears or holes, use your fingers to gently squeeze the dough back together.

Funny Bunny
QUESADILLA

Hop to it! Here's a single-serve snack to make you smile!
Bonus: Fill a paper cup with our DIY Hummus (page 70) and add a few baby carrots!

1. Place handful (about 2 tablespoons) of **shredded cheese** in center of **round flour tortilla**. Fold bottom up about a third of the way.

2. Fold in right side, then left, forming square bottom.

3. Hold at folds and use kitchen scissors to cut two slits, about 1 inch apart, on round side, forming "ears" with flap between them.

4. Lower flap to meet square edge. Lightly toast on a tray in toaster oven until cheese melts. Add **cherry-tomato** nose, **carrot** eyes, **chive** whiskers, **celery** mouth, and **red-onion** or **cabbage** ear accents.

DIY
HUMMUS

Why settle for store-bought dip when it's so much tastier to do it yourself?
If not serving right away, cover and refrigerate for up to 3 days.

TOTAL TIME → 15 MINUTES   MAKES → 1½ CUPS

INGREDIENTS

1 lemon

1 can (15 ounces)
garbanzo beans, rinsed
and drained

2 tablespoons tahini
(sesame seed paste)

3 tablespoons olive oil

1 small garlic clove

pinch of cayenne
pepper

¼ teaspoon salt

pita chips, for serving

EACH TABLESPOON

Calories: About 35
Protein: 1G
Carbohydrates: 4G
Total Fat: 2G
(Saturated Fat: 0G)
Fiber: 1G
Sodium: 65MG

1. From lemon, grate 1 teaspoon peel and squeeze 2 tablespoons juice.

2. In food processor with knife blade attached, process lemon peel and juice, beans, tahini, oil, 2 tablespoons water, garlic, cayenne pepper, and salt until smooth.

3. Serve with pita chips.

Cauliflower "POPCORN"

Try these healthy munchies next time you stream a movie!

ACTIVE TIME → 10 MINUTES   **TOTAL TIME** → 35 MINUTES   **MAKES** → 5 CUPS

INGREDIENTS

8 cups small cauliflower florets (about 1¼ pounds), stems trimmed

3 tablespoons olive oil

½ teaspoon salt

EACH CUP
Calories: About 135
Protein: 4G
Carbohydrates: 9G
Total Fat: 9G
(Saturated Fat: 1G)
Fiber: 3G
Sodium: 356MG

1. Preheat oven to 475°F.

2. On large rimmed baking sheet, toss cauliflower florets, oil, and salt. Roast for 25 to 30 minutes or until browned and tender. Serve immediately.

→ ## Parmesan

Prepare recipe as directed, but add ¼ **cup grated Parmesan cheese, 1 teaspoon garlic powder**, and **½ teaspoon turmeric** to the oil mixture.

→ ## Chili-Lime

Prepare recipe as directed, but add **1 teaspoon chili powder** to the oil mixture. **Grate zest of 1 lime** over roasted cauliflower before serving.

SMART CHEF! Leftover cauliflower stems? Peel and slice them to serve with our DIY Hummus (left).

FUN FOOD!

VEGGIE ROLLS

Enjoy your fruits and veggies sushi-style!
The rolls can stand at room temperature up to 1 hour.

1. In large bowl, combine **1 package (8 ounces) cream cheese**, softened; ⅛ **teaspoon salt**; and desired flavorings (right). Cut 3 cups desired sliced vegetables and/or fruit (right) into 2-inch-long matchsticks.

2. With vegetable peeler, shave **zucchini or yellow squash** into 16 wide ribbons. Stop peeling when you reach seeds; discard the seeds.

3. Spread 1 tablespoon flavored cream cheese on one side of veggie ribbon. Add veggie/ fruit sticks from the combos given (right), arranging so the tops stick out to one side.

4. Starting with the veggie/fruit, roll the ribbon and continue rolling until there is no ribbon left and the roll looks like a piece of sushi. The cream cheese will act like glue and hold everything together.

Red Pepper-Basil

Add ⅓ cup finely chopped **roasted red peppers** to cream cheese mixture. Fill with **fresh basil leaves** and **sliced bell pepper** and **green apple** sticks.

EACH ROLL: About 65 Calories, 1G Protein, 4G Carbohydrate, 5G Total Fat (3G Saturated), 1G Fiber, 80MG Sodium

Asian Garden

Add **1 tablespoon soy sauce** and **2 teaspoons fresh lime juice** to cream cheese mixture. Fill with **radish, green onion,** and **carrot** sticks.

EACH ROLL: About 55 Calories, 1G Protein, 3G Carbohydrate, 5G Total Fat (3G Saturated), 1G Fiber, 131MG Sodium

Veggie Chili

Add ½ **cup shredded cheddar cheese** and **1 teaspoon chili powder** to cream cheese mixture. Fill with **fresh cilantro sprigs** and **cucumber** and **jicama** sticks.

EACH ROLL: About 75 Calories, 2G Protein, 3G Carbohydrate, 6G Total Fat (4G Saturated), 1G Fiber, 93MG Sodium

Zippy Pear

Add 1½ **tablespoons horseradish** to cream cheese mixture. Fill with **fresh parsley sprigs** and **pear** and **celery** sticks.

EACH ROLL: About 60 Calories, 1G Protein, 4G Carbohydrate, 5G Total Fat (3G Saturated), 1G Fiber, 78MG Sodium

Smoky
GUACAMOLE

Holy moly, wait 'til you taste this guacamole! The secret? Pan-grilled avocados.
Use avocados with thick, pebbly, green skin like Hass, Pinkerton, or Reed.

ACTIVE TIME → 10 MINUTES   TOTAL TIME → 15 MINUTES   MAKES → ABOUT 1¼ CUPS

INGREDIENTS

2 ripe avocados, halved
and pitted

2 teaspoons vegetable oil

3 tablespoons fresh lime
juice

1 garlic clove, crushed
with press

½ teaspoon salt

¼ to ½ teaspoon ground
chipotle chile

¼ cup finely chopped red
onion

¼ cup finely chopped
fresh cilantro

tortilla chips, for serving

EACH ½ CUP

Calories: About 190
Protein: 2G
Carbohydrates: 11G
Total Fat: 17G
(Saturated Fat: 2G)
Fiber: 7G
Sodium: 265MG

1. Heat large ridged grill pan over medium-high heat until hot.

2. Brush cut sides of avocados with oil. Place avocados, cut-side down, in grill pan, and cook for 2 to 4 minutes or until grill marks appear.

3. Transfer avocados to cutting board; cool slightly. Remove avocados from peel. Mash with lime juice, garlic, salt, and chipotle until almost smooth. Stir in onion and cilantro.

4. Transfer guacamole to serving bowl. Cover and refrigerate for about 1 hour or until cold. Serve with tortilla chips.

?

WHAT IS IT?

A **RIDGED GRILL PAN** is a skillet (or griddle) with raised ridges that look like the bars of a grilling rack. The best pans are made from cast iron.

FUN FOOD!

Snack
CLASSICS

These two recipes work great as snacks or as part of a larger meal.

Green Onion Yogurt Dip

In large skillet, heat **2 teaspoons olive oil** over medium heat until hot. Add **1 bunch green onions**, thinly sliced, and **1 garlic clove**, chopped. Cook for about 5 minutes or until golden, stirring. Cool completely. In food processor with knife blade attached, puree onion mixture, **1½ cups nonfat Greek yogurt**, **½ cup reduced-fat mayonnaise**, **1 tablespoon fresh lemon juice**, **¼ teaspoon paprika**, and **¼ teaspoon salt**. Refrigerate until cold or up to 3 days. Serve with veggies or pretzels. Makes about 2 cups.

EACH ¼ CUP: About 65 Calories, 4G Protein, 5G Carbohydrate, 3G Total Fat (1G Saturated), 1G Fiber, 220MG Sodium

Sweet & Savory Snack Mix

Preheat oven to 275°F. In small saucepan, mix **4 tablespoons butter**, **3 tablespoons honey**, **3 tablespoons soy sauce**, and **2 teaspoons freshly grated lime peel**. Cook over medium heat for 2 minutes or until butter melts, stirring. In large bowl, combine **4 cups unsweetened shredded wheat squares**; **2 cups whole-grain crackers**, broken up; **1 cup roasted salted edamame**; and **1 cup roasted salted cashews**. Drizzle with butter mixture; toss well. Transfer to 2 large rimmed baking sheets. Bake for 30 minutes or until golden, stirring and rotating pans halfway through. Cool completely. Can be stored in airtight container up to 3 weeks. Makes about 7 cups.

EACH ½ CUP: About 235 Calories, 9G Protein, 27G Carbohydrate, 12G Total Fat (4G Saturated), 5G Fiber, 335MG Sodium

FUN FOOD!

Treat
YOURSELF!

You'll love this recipe trio—it's the perfect combination for a party or even just a small get-together with friends! Note: for the Parsnip Chips, be sure to ask an adult to help slice the veggies.

Pineapple & Toasted-Coconut Skewers

Thread ½ cup pineapple chunks onto skewers. Sprinkle with pinch of ground cinnamon. Top with 1 tablespoon toasted coconut chips and 10 cashews. Serves 1.

EACH SERVING: About 155 Calories, 3G Protein, 18G Carbohydrate, 9G Total Fat (3G Saturated), 2G Fiber, 30MG Sodium

Spiced Apple Wedges with Yogurt

Preheat oven to 375°F. On small rimmed baking sheet, toss 2 medium apples, thinly sliced; 2 teaspoons grated peeled fresh ginger; and ½ teaspoon ground cinnamon. Roast for 20 minutes or until tender. Serve with dollop of low-fat vanilla yogurt. Serves 2.

EACH SERVING: About 140 Calories, 3G Protein, 30G Carbohydrate, 1G Total Fat (0G Saturated), 2G Fiber, 30MG Sodium

Parsnip Chips

Preheat oven to 275°F. Line large cookie sheet with foil. Very thinly slice 8 ounces large parsnips into rounds. Toss with 1 tablespoon olive oil, ⅛ teaspoon salt, and ⅛ teaspoon ground black pepper. Arrange in single layer on cookie sheet. Bake for 50 to 55 minutes or until brown and curled. Let stand at least 10 minutes before serving. Serves 2.

EACH SERVING: About 130 Calories, 1G Protein, 17G Carbohydrate, 7G Total Fat (1G Saturated), 5G Fiber, 155MG Sodium

Apple
DOUGHNUTS

We bet you've never eaten apples like this before! Just core, slice into horizontal rings, and top with "frosting" (like nut butter or cream cheese) and "sprinkles" (like fruit, coconut, marshmallows, nuts, or seeds). With dozens of delicious combos, you won't miss the fried dough.

→ **Greek Yogurt + Lemon Zest + Honey + Poppy Seeds**

→ **Blueberry Cream Cheese + Blueberries**

→ **Cheesecake Filling + Pistachios + Dried Lavender**

→ **Strawberry Cream Cheese + Granola + Strawberries**

→ **Chocolate-Hazelnut Spread + Coconut + Marshmallows**

→ **Peanut Butter + Banana + Chocolate**

Iced Tea
WITH FRUIT JUICE

The next time you're parched, try one of these super thirst quenchers!
Be sure to use non-caffeinated tea—it'll help you relax!

TOTAL TIME → 10 MINUTES   MAKES → 8 SERVINGS (8 CUPS)

INGREDIENTS

4 cups peach or apricot
juice/nectar, or lemonade

8 tea bags of choice

ice cubes

granulated or superfine
sugar, optional

thin lemon slices,
optional

EACH SERVING

Calories: About 60
Protein: 0G
Carbohydrates: 17G
Total Fat: 0G
(Saturated Fat: 0G)
Fiber: 0G
Sodium: 14MG

1. In nonreactive 3-quart saucepan, heat juice to boiling over high heat. Remove from heat and stir in tea bags. Cover and steep 5 minutes.

2. Stir again and remove tea bags. Pour tea into heatproof 2½-quart pitcher. Add 4 cups cold water. Cover and let stand until ready to serve.

3. Fill tall glasses with ice cubes and pour tea over. Serve with sugar and lemon slices, if using.

FUN FOOD!

BEST-EVER
HOT COCOA

On a cold day, hot chocolate is like comfort in a cup. We've created the ultimate recipe for chocolate-y goodness, plus three yummy variations. Don't forget to add a dollop of whipped cream on top!

TOTAL TIME → 10 MINUTES   MAKES → ABOUT 3½ CUPS

INGREDIENTS

1½ cups unsweetened cocoa

1¼ cups sugar

6 ounces semisweet chocolate, coarsely chopped

¼ teaspoon salt

Whole milk

1. In food processor with knife blade attached, process cocoa, sugar, chocolate, and salt until almost smooth. Store in tightly sealed container at room temperature for up to 6 months.

2. For each serving, combine 3 tablespoons cocoa mix and 1 cup milk in a microwave-safe mug. Microwave on High for 1½ to 2 minutes or until blended and hot, stirring once.

Mocha Hot Cocoa

Prepare hot cocoa as directed, but add ⅓ **cup instant coffee powder or granules** before blending in processor.

EACH SERVING: About 115 Calories, 2G Protein, 22G Carbohydrate, 4G Total Fat (2G Saturated), 3G Fiber, 35MG Sodium

Mexican Hot Cocoa

Prepare hot cocoa as directed, but add **2 teaspoons ground cinnamon** and ¼ **teaspoon cayenne pepper** before blending in processor.

EACH SERVING: About 115 Calories, 2G Protein, 22G Carbohydrate, 4G Total Fat (2G Saturated), 3G Fiber, 35MG Sodium

Vanilla Hot Cocoa

Prepare hot cocoa as directed, but add ½ **vanilla bean** (pod and seeds) before blending in processor.

EACH SERVING: About 115 Calories, 2G Protein, 22G Carbohydrate, 4G Total Fat (2G Saturated), 3G Fiber, 35MG Sodium

Strawberry
LEMONADE

The right mix of sweet, sour, and refreshing, this drink will
bring you cool relief on those hot summer days.

TOTAL TIME → 15 MINUTES (PLUS CHILLING)   MAKES → 8 SERVINGS

INGREDIENTS

12 ounces strawberries,
hulled (2 cups)

2 quarts store-bought
lemonade

EACH SERVING

Calories: About 115
Protein: 0G
Carbohydrates: 28G
Total Fat: 0G
(Saturated Fat: 0G)
Fiber: 0G
Sodium: 40MG

1. In blender, puree strawberries. Strain through fine-mesh sieve set over a
medium-size bowl. You should end up with about 1 cup strained puree.

2. In large pitcher, stir lemonade and puree until blended. Cover and
refrigerate until chilled, at least 30 minutes.

SMART CHEF! Hull strawberries an easier way: Insert a plastic straw
through the bottom center of the fruit, then push out the green stem.
Done!

Fizzy Cranberry-
LEMONADE PUNCH

This punch is perfect for pool parties and summer cookouts with friends and family.

TOTAL TIME → 10 MINUTES   MAKES → 12 SERVINGS

INGREDIENTS

4 cups cranberry-juice cocktail, chilled

1 container (6 ounces) frozen lemonade concentrate, thawed

1 bottle (1 liter) plain seltzer or club soda, chilled

ice cubes, optional

1 small orange, cut into ¼-inch-thick slices and each slice cut in half

EACH SERVING

Calories: About 80
Protein: 0G
Carbohydrates: 21G
Total Fat: 0G
(Saturated Fat: 0G)
Fiber: 0G
Sodium: 23MG

1. In large pitcher, stir cranberry-juice cocktail and lemonade concentrate until blended. Stir in seltzer and ice cubes, if using. Add orange slices and serve.

4

Tasty Dinners & Sides

Attention, young chefs! Making dinner is your time to shine.
We've got dynamite mains and sides for every level—from hot dogs, tacos, and
corn on the cob for beginners to dressed up mac 'n' cheese, fish 'n' chips, and DIY pizza for
more seasoned cooks. Get ready—tonight, you're getting a standing ovation!

Sausage-Stuffed
ZUCCHINI BOATS

Serve this hearty stuffed veggie with a side of cooked penne or ziti.

ACTIVE TIME → 15 MINUTES   TOTAL TIME → 1 HOUR   MAKES → 4 SERVINGS

INGREDIENTS

4 small zucchini

2 teaspoons olive oil

1 small onion, chopped

2 links sweet Italian sausage, casings removed

¼ teaspoon salt

1¼ cups marinara sauce

4 ounces shredded mozzarella cheese (½ cup)

chopped fresh parsley, for garnish

EACH SERVING

Calories: About 325
Protein: 16G
Carbohydrates: 15G
Total Fat: 23G
(Saturated Fat: 9G)
Fiber: 3G
Sodium: 925MG

1. Preheat oven to 450°F. Spray 3-quart baking dish with nonstick cooking spray.

2. Cut 4 small zucchini lengthwise in half. With small metal spoon, scrape out insides, leaving ¼-inch shell. Chop insides.

3. In 10-inch skillet, heat oil over medium-high heat until hot. Add chopped zucchini, onion, sausage, and salt. Cook, stirring and breaking up sausage with side of spoon, for 8 minutes or until sausage is cooked through.

4. Spread marinara sauce in bottom of prepared baking dish. Arrange zucchini shells on top, cut sides up. Spoon sausage mixture into shells. Top evenly with mozzarella. Cover with foil. Bake for 30 minutes. Uncover; bake for 5 minutes longer or until cheese browns. Garnish with parsley.

Spaghetti
BOLOGNESE

Unlike classic Bolognese sauce, which takes hours to cook,
this recipe is ready in a fraction of the time.

ACTIVE TIME → 15 MINUTES   TOTAL TIME → 40 MINUTES   MAKES → 6 SERVINGS

INGREDIENTS

1 tablespoon olive oil

1 medium onion, chopped

3 garlic cloves, chopped

½ teaspoon salt

1 pound ground beef chuck

1 can (28 ounces) crushed tomatoes

2 tablespoons grated pecorino cheese

½ cup milk

1 pound spaghetti

fresh basil leaves and grated pecorino cheese, optional

EACH SERVING

Calories: About 575
Protein: 27G
Carbohydrates: 21G
Total Fat: 21G
(Saturated Fat: 7G)
Fiber: 6G
Sodium: 485MG

1. In large saucepot, heat oil over medium-high heat until hot. Add onion, garlic, and salt; cook for 10 minutes or until tender, stirring occasionally. Add beef. Cook, stirring and breaking up beef with side of spoon, for 5 minutes or until beef loses its pink color throughout. Add tomatoes; heat to boiling over high heat. Reduce heat and simmer for 10 minutes or until flavors are blended. Stir in pecorino and milk.

2. Meanwhile, cook pasta as label directs. Drain.

3. Add pasta to sauce, tossing to combine. Garnish with basil leaves and more pecorino, if using.

Beef 'N' Mushroom
BURGERS

Mushrooms, with their surprisingly meaty taste, make these cheeseburgers extra juicy.
Choose cremini mushrooms for even richer flavor.

ACTIVE TIME → 15 MINUTES   TOTAL TIME → 25 MINUTES   MAKES → 4 SERVINGS

INGREDIENTS

8 ounces mushrooms

1 tablespoon
Worcestershire sauce

12 ounces ground beef
sirloin (90%)

¼ cup grated onion,
squeezed dry

¼ teaspoon ground black
pepper

1 tablespoon vegetable oil

4 slices American cheese
or cheddar cheese (about
3 ounces)

4 hamburger buns, split
and toasted

lettuce leaves and
tomato slices

EACH SERVING

Calories: About 350
Protein: 27G
Carbohydrates: 28G
Total Fat: 14G
(Saturated Fat: 6G)
Fiber: 2G
Sodium: 660MG

1. In food processor with knife blade attached, pulse mushrooms and
Worcestershire until mushrooms are finely chopped.

2. In large bowl, combine mushroom mixture, beef, and onion until blended,
but do not overmix.

3. Shape meat mixture into 4 equal patties, each about 4 inches wide,
handling meat as little as possible. Sprinkle pepper on both sides of patties.

4. In 12-inch nonstick skillet, heat oil over medium heat until hot. Add
patties. Cook for 5 minutes. Turn patties over; increase heat to medium-high.
Top each patty with 1 slice cheese. Cook for 4 minutes or until cheese melts.

5. Serve burgers on buns with lettuce and tomato.

SMART CHEF! Use a gentle touch when shaping burgers (and
meatballs, too). Tightly packing them makes the meat dry out
during cooking.

Taco DOGS

Chili dogs go taco-style thanks to our additions of salsa verde, crushed tortilla chips, and crisp lettuce.

ACTIVE TIME → 5 MINUTES   **TOTAL TIME →** 20 MINUTES   **MAKES →** 6 SERVINGS

INGREDIENTS

6 all-beef hot dogs

2 teaspoons vegetable oil

8 ounces ground beef sirloin (85%)

1 tablespoon chili powder

½ cup salsa verde

6 hot dog buns, split and toasted

3 ounces shredded cheddar cheese (¾ cup)

¾ cup crushed tortilla chips

shredded lettuce

EACH SERVING

Calories: About 435
Protein: 20G
Carbohydrates: 29G
Total Fat: 26G
(Saturated Fat: 10G)
Fiber: 2G
Sodium: 1,000MG

1. Set ridged grill pan over medium heat until hot.

2. Place hot dogs on hot grill pan; cook for 7 to 9 minutes or until heated through (meaning every part of the meat is cooked), turning occasionally.

3. Meanwhile, in 10-inch skillet, heat oil over medium-high heat until hot. Add beef and chili powder. Cook, stirring and breaking up beef with side of spoon, for 3 to 4 minutes or until beef loses its pink color throughout. Stir in salsa. Cook for 1 minute longer or until heated through.

4. Place hot dogs in buns; top evenly with beef mixture. Top each hot dog with 3 tablespoons cheddar, 3 tablespoons tortilla chips, and lettuce.

Steak
& FINGERLING FRIES

Slender fingerling potatoes look like—you guessed it—fingers! Firm in texture with a flavor that ranges from mildly sweet to rich and nutty, these spuds are also an excellent choice for making crispy oven fries.

ACTIVE TIME → 10 MINUTES   TOTAL TIME → 20 MINUTES   MAKES → 4 SERVINGS

INGREDIENTS

1 pound fingerling potatoes, quartered lengthwise

2 tablespoons olive oil

¾ teaspoon salt

2 tablespoons butter, softened

1 tablespoon prepared pesto

2 boneless top loin beef steaks, 1¼ pounds (each 1 inch thick)

½ teaspoon ground black pepper

EACH SERVING

Calories: About 425
Protein: 33G
Carbohydrates: 21G
Total Fat: 23G
(Saturated Fat: 8G)
Fiber: 3G
Sodium: 520MG

1. Preheat oven to 450°F.

2. On large rimmed baking sheet, combine potatoes, 1 tablespoon oil, and ¼ teaspoon salt; tossing to coat. Bake for 20 minutes or until deep golden brown.

3. Meanwhile, in small bowl, combine butter and pesto.

4. Sprinkle steaks with remaining ½ teaspoon salt and pepper. In 12-inch skillet, heat remaining 1 tablespoon oil over medium-high heat until hot. Add steaks. Cook for about 6 minutes for medium-rare or until desired doneness, turning over once. Transfer steaks to cutting board. Let stand 5 minutes to set juices for easier slicing.

5. Slice steaks across grain. Serve with pesto butter and fries.

SMART CHEF! What does slicing steak "across the grain" mean? Look closely and you'll notice long lines at the top of the steak—these are muscle fibers running through the meat. If you slice in the same direction as the lines, you'll have to chew through the tough fibers. But slice steak across the grain, and you'll create smaller fibers, so your steak will be tender.

Meatball-Mozzarella PIZZA

What's more fun than make-it-yourself pizza?
Topping it with tiny homemade meatballs!

ACTIVE TIME → 15 MINUTES   TOTAL TIME → 35 MINUTES   MAKES → 6 SERVINGS

INGREDIENTS

1¼ pounds fresh
or frozen (thawed)
pizza dough, at room
temperature

4 ounces shredded
mozzarella cheese
(½ cup)

2 plum tomatoes, thinly
sliced

½ small red onion, thinly
sliced

¼ teaspoon ground black
pepper

8 ounces ground beef
chuck or ground turkey

¼ cup Italian-seasoned
bread crumbs

pinch of salt

EACH SERVING

Calories: About 395
Protein: 18G
Carbohydrates: 48G
Total Fat: 13G
(Saturated Fat: 5G)
Fiber: 2G
Sodium: 1,130MG

1. Place large cookie sheet in oven; preheat oven to 450°F.

2. On large sheet parchment paper, stretch and roll dough into 13-inch circle. Top with mozzarella, tomatoes, onion, and pepper.

3. In large bowl, combine beef, bread crumbs, and salt, but do not overmix. Shape into 1-inch meatballs.

4. Place meatballs on pizza. Spray pizza with nonstick cooking spray. Carefully slide pizza on parchment onto preheated cookie sheet. Bake for 20 to 25 minutes, or until bottom of crust is deep golden brown.

SMART CHEF! Customize your meatball pizza by changing toppings—we used Italian-blend cheese, marinara sauce, and an assortment of veggies to make the pizza on the cover. Yum!

Classic Chicken
PARMESAN

Seasoned bread crumbs and store-bought marinara sauce makes prepping this dish easy and quick.

ACTIVE TIME → 20 MINUTES   TOTAL TIME → 50 MINUTES   MAKES → 4 SERVINGS

INGREDIENTS

½ cup Italian-seasoned bread crumbs

½ cup grated Parmesan cheese

2 large eggs

4 small chicken-breast halves (about 1½ pounds)

3 tablespoons olive oil

¾ cup marinara sauce

6 ounces shredded mozzarella cheese (¾ cup)

crusty bread, optional

EACH SERVING

Calories: About 515
Protein: 50G
Carbohydrates: 18G
Total Fat: 26G
(Saturated Fat: 9G)
Fiber: 1G
Sodium: 1,170MG

1. Preheat oven to 450°F. Spray baking dish with nonstick cooking spray.

2. On medium plate, combine bread crumbs and Parmesan. In shallow bowl, with fork, beat eggs.

3. Dip chicken in egg. Coat with crumb mixture, firmly pressing so mixture adheres.

4. In 12-inch skillet, heat oil over medium-high heat until hot. Add chicken; fry for 7 minutes or until golden brown, turning over once.

5. Transfer chicken to prepared baking dish. Top with marinara sauce and mozzarella. Bake for 20 minutes or until chicken is no longer pink throughout and sauce is bubbling. Serve with crusty bread, if using.

SMART CHEF! The trick for shredding softer cheeses like mozzarella, Jack, and even cheddar is to spray the front and back of the grater with nonstick cooking spray (or rub those surfaces with an oil-coated paper towel) before grating. To get the best-looking shreds, freeze soft cheeses for 30 minutes beforehand.

Pecorino
CHICKEN FINGERS

Typical fast-food fare gets a tasty makeover—and it's better for you, too!

ACTIVE TIME → 20 MINUTES   TOTAL TIME → 30 MINUTES   MAKES → 4 SERVINGS

INGREDIENTS

1 cup panko bread crumbs, toasted

⅓ cup grated pecorino cheese

¼ teaspoon salt

⅛ to ¼ teaspoon cayenne pepper

2 large egg whites

1 garlic clove, crushed with press

1½ pounds chicken tenders

1 cup marinara sauce

¼ cup loosely packed fresh basil leaves, chopped

EACH SERVING

Calories: About 345
Protein: 43G
Carbohydrates: 20G
Total Fat: 8G
(Saturated Fat: 3G)
Fiber: 0G
Sodium: 746MG

1. Preheat oven to 475°F. Place wire rack in large rimmed baking sheet; spray pan and wire rack with olive oil cooking spray.

2. On medium plate, combine panko, pecorino, salt, and cayenne. In shallow bowl with wire whisk, beat egg whites and garlic until well mixed.

3. One at a time, dip chicken tenders in egg-white mixture. Coat with panko mixture, firmly pressing so mixture adheres. Arrange chicken on prepared rack in pan. Spray chicken lightly with olive oil cooking spray.

4. Bake for 10 to 12 minutes or until crust is golden brown and chicken is no longer pink throughout.

5. Meanwhile, in 1-quart saucepot, cook marinara sauce over medium to low heat for 5 minutes or until hot, stirring occasionally. Remove saucepot from heat and stir in basil. Serve as dipping sauce with chicken.

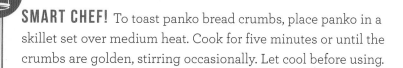

SMART CHEF! To toast panko bread crumbs, place panko in a skillet set over medium heat. Cook for five minutes or until the crumbs are golden, stirring occasionally. Let cool before using.

Lemon-Rosemary
CHICKEN & POTATOES

Cooking chicken thighs in individual foil packets keeps the meat juicy while also sealing in the flavor.

ACTIVE TIME → 15 MINUTES   TOTAL TIME → 45 MINUTES   MAKES → 4 SERVINGS

INGREDIENTS

4 medium red potatoes, thinly sliced

salt

4 large skinless, boneless chicken thighs

¼ cup (½ stick) butter, melted

½ teaspoon ground black pepper

1 large lemon, thinly sliced

4 teaspoons chopped fresh rosemary

EACH SERVING

Calories: About 370
Protein: 21G
Carbohydrates: 36G
Total Fat: 16G
(Saturated Fat: 8G)
Fiber: 4G
Sodium: 925MG

1. Preheat oven to 425°F.

2. Tear four (18-by-12-inch) sheets of foil. For each packet, place 1 piece of foil on cutting board with longer side of foil facing you. Arrange one-quarter of potatoes, overlapping slightly in center of foil; top with pinch of salt and 1 chicken thigh. Drizzle with 1 tablespoon butter; sprinkle with ¼ teaspoon salt and ¼ teaspoon pepper. Top with one quarter of lemon slices and 1 teaspoon rosemary. Fold foil around chicken and vegetables; tightly crimp the edges to form total of 4 packets.

3. Place packets on large cookie sheet. Bake 30 for minutes or until potatoes are tender. Open packets carefully, allowing steam to escape.

SMART CHEF! Be sure to wear potholders when unwrapping the packets. The steam inside will be hot, hot, hot!

BBQ Chicken
TACOS

Fresh corn kernels make these tacos extra tasty. If corn is not in season, swap in an equal amount of thawed frozen corn.

TOTAL TIME → 15 MINUTES   MAKES → 4 SERVINGS

INGREDIENTS

2 cups shredded rotisserie chicken meat

⅓ cup barbecue sauce

1½ cups corn kernels cut from cobs (about 3 ears)

2 plum tomatoes, chopped

1 tablespoon fresh lime juice

8 soft taco-size flour tortillas

3 cups thinly sliced iceberg lettuce

½ cup light sour cream

EACH SERVING

Calories: About 480
Protein: 30G
Carbohydrates: 58G
Total Fat: 15G
(Saturated Fat: 5G)
Fiber: 5G
Sodium: 705MG

1. In large bowl, combine chicken, barbecue sauce, corn, tomatoes, and lime juice.

2. Place stack of tortillas between paper towels on microwave-safe plate. Microwave on High for 10 to 15 seconds or until warm.

3. Divide lettuce and chicken mixture among warm tortillas; fold over to eat out of hand. Serve with sour cream.

Crunchy
DEVILED CHICKEN

We love working with chicken thighs because they're juicier, more flavorful, and less likely to overcook than chicken breasts. The juiciness goes great with the crunch of panko bread crumbs.

ACTIVE TIME → 10 MINUTES   TOTAL TIME → 30 MINUTES   MAKES → 4 SERVINGS

INGREDIENTS

1¼ cups panko bread crumbs

3 tablespoons spicy brown mustard

1 large egg

½ teaspoon smoked paprika

1¼ pounds skinless, boneless chicken thighs

1 pound medium carrots, halved lengthwise

½ teaspoon salt

salad greens

EACH SERVING

Calories: About 355
Protein: 30G
Carbohydrates: 31G
Total Fat: 10G
(Saturated Fat: 3G)
Fiber: 4G
Sodium: 605MG

1. Preheat oven to 450°F. Spray 2 rimmed baking sheets with nonstick cooking spray.

2. On medium plate, spread panko. In shallow bowl with wire whisk, combine mustard, egg, and paprika until blended.

3. Dip chicken in egg mixture. Coat with panko, firmly pressing to adhere. Place on 1 prepared baking sheet. On other prepared baking sheet, arrange carrots.

4. Spray chicken and carrots with nonstick cooking spray; sprinkle with salt. Bake for 20 minutes or until carrots are tender and chicken is no longer pink throughout. Serve over salad greens.

Triple-Decker
TORTILLA PIE

Here's a great way to use rotisserie chicken from the supermarket.
If you like your Tex-Mex on the spicy side, swap in Pepper Jack cheese.

ACTIVE TIME → 15 MINUTES   TOTAL TIME → 25 MINUTES   MAKES → 4 SERVINGS

INGREDIENTS

1 (2- to 2½-pound) rotisserie chicken

1 can (12 ounces) enchilada sauce

3 burrito-size flour tortillas

4 ounces shredded Monterey Jack cheese (½ cup)

shredded romaine lettuce, halved cherry tomatoes, and diced avocado, for garnish

EACH SERVING
WITHOUT GARNISHES

Calories: About 550
Protein: 48G
Carbohydrates: 33G
Total Fat: 24G
(Saturated Fat: 9G)
Fiber: 2G
Sodium: 980MG

1. Preheat oven to 450°F.

2. Remove skin and bones from chicken; shred meat. In medium bowl, combine chicken and enchilada sauce.

3. Place 1 flour tortilla in 10- to 12-inch skillet. Top with half of chicken mixture and ⅓ cup Monterey Jack cheese. Repeat with 1 tortilla, remaining chicken mixture, and ⅓ cup cheese. Top with remaining tortilla and remaining ⅓ cup cheese.

4. Bake for 8 to 10 minutes or until heated through and cheese has melted. Garnish with lettuce, tomatoes, and avocado.

Fish 'N' CHIPS

Our clever potato-chip coating means you don't have to fry the fillets to make them extra crispy.

ACTIVE TIME → 20 MINUTES   TOTAL TIME → 30 MINUTES   MAKES → 4 SERVINGS

INGREDIENTS

1 bag (6 ounces) salt-and-vinegar potato chips, finely crushed

3 large egg whites

1½ pounds cod fillets, cut into strips

½ teaspoon salt

1 pound frozen peas

3 tablespoons butter

1 tablespoon fresh lemon juice

¼ teaspoon ground black pepper

lemon wedges and snipped fresh chives, for garnish

EACH SERVING

Calories: About 295
Protein: 35G
Carbohydrates: 16G
Total Fat: 10G
(Saturated Fat: 6G)
Fiber: 6G
Sodium: 570MG

1. Preheat oven to 450°F. Line large baking sheet with foil; spray generously with nonstick spray.

2. On medium plate, spread potato chips. In pie plate with fork, beat egg whites.

3. Working in batches, dip cod in egg. Coat with potato chips, firmly pressing so potato chips stick to egg. Arrange cod on prepared pan; spray with nonstick cooking spray. Bake for 12 minutes or until cod is white throughout. Sprinkle with ¼ teaspoon salt.

4. Meanwhile, in large microwave-safe bowl, combine peas, butter, lemon juice, remaining ¼ teaspoon salt, and pepper. Cover with vented microwave-safe plastic wrap (i.e., with a corner of the wrap left open so steam can escape); microwave on High for 5 minutes or until hot. In food processor with knife blade attached, pulse pea mixture until smooth.

5. Serve cod with peas; garnish with lemon wedges and chives.

SMART CHEF! Crush the potato chips right in the bag! Make a small hole in the top, and then go to town with a rolling pin.

Garlic-Shrimp
CAESAR SALAD

Lemony roasted shrimp makes this classic salad dinner-worthy.
Buy peeled and deveined shrimp (versus in-shell) to make prep easy.

ACTIVE TIME → 10 MINUTES   TOTAL TIME → 30 MINUTES   MAKES → 4 SERVINGS

INGREDIENTS

1 pound peeled and
deveined medium shrimp

2 tablespoons olive oil

4 tablespoons fresh
lemon juice

4 garlic cloves

2 teaspoons Dijon
mustard

1 teaspoon paprika

¼ cup plain nonfat Greek
yogurt

3 tablespoons grated
Parmesan cheese

¼ teaspoon salt

¼ teaspoon ground
black pepper

1 head romaine lettuce

1 heart radicchio, sliced

1 cup croutons

EACH SERVING

Calories: About 240
Protein: 22G
Carbohydrates: 17G
Total Fat: 10G
(Saturated Fat: 2G)
Fiber: 4G
Sodium: 910MG

1. Preheat oven to 400°F. Line large cookie sheet with foil.

2. In large bowl, combine shrimp, oil, 1 tablespoon lemon juice, 3 garlic cloves crushed through press, mustard, and paprika, tossing to coat. Refrigerate for 10 minutes.

3. Meanwhile, in large serving bowl, with wire whisk, mix yogurt, remaining 3 tablespoons lemon juice, Parmesan, remaining garlic clove crushed through press, salt, and pepper until blended.

4. Spread shrimp on prepared cookie sheet. Roast for 10 minutes or until pink.

5. Add chopped romaine and radicchio to serving bowl; toss to coat with dressing. Top with shrimp and croutons.

Hoisin-Glazed
SALMON

We packed this zippy salmon dish in foil packets to keep the
fish ultra-moist and the cleanup extra easy.

ACTIVE TIME ➔ 20 MINUTES   TOTAL TIME ➔ 35 MINUTES   MAKES ➔ 4 SERVINGS

INGREDIENTS

4 salmon fillets
(6 ounces each), skin
removed

1 tablespoon hoisin sauce

crushed red pepper
(optional)

1½ pounds cauliflower
florets

1 tablespoon vegetable
oil

¼ teaspoon salt

¼ cup chopped peanuts

¼ cup chopped fresh
cilantro

EACH SERVING

Calories: About 410
Protein: 43G
Carbohydrates: 18G
Total Fat: 19G
(Saturated Fat: 3G)
Fiber: 5G
Sodium: 535MG

1. Preheat oven to 425°F.

2. Tear four (18-by-12-inch) sheets of foil. For each packet, place 1 piece foil
on cutting board with longer side of foil facing you. Place 1 salmon fillet in
center of each. Brush each fillet with 1 tablespoon hoisin sauce and sprinkle
with pinch of crushed red pepper, if using.

3. In large bowl, combine cauliflower, oil, and salt, tossing to coat. Arrange
cauliflower around each fillet. Fold foil around salmon and vegetables;
tightly crimp the edges to form total of 4 packets.

4. Place packets on large cookie sheet. Bake for 15 minutes or until
cauliflower is tender. Open packets carefully, allowing steam to escape.
Garnish with peanuts and cilantro.

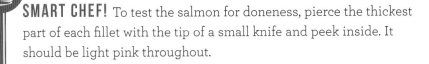

SMART CHEF! To test the salmon for doneness, pierce the thickest
part of each fillet with the tip of a small knife and peek inside. It
should be light pink throughout.

Lo Mein
WITH STIR-FRY VEGETABLES

You've probably had lo mein at a restaurant, but now you can make it at home!
This comfort food fave will impress everyone at the table.

ACTIVE TIME → 10 MINUTES   TOTAL TIME → 35 MINUTES   MAKES → 4 SERVINGS

INGREDIENTS

8 ounces linguine or spaghetti

2 tablespoons vegetable oil

1 pound ground chicken

⅛ teaspoon salt

1 garlic clove, crushed with press

2 green onions, thinly sliced (reserve dark-green tops for garnish)

1 package (10 ounces) sliced mushrooms

½ small head napa cabbage, thinly sliced (5 cups)

1½ cups shredded carrots (half of 10-ounce bag)

¼ cup teriyaki sauce

1 tablespoon grated, peeled fresh ginger

EACH SERVING

Calories: About 560
Protein: 32G
Carbohydrates: 56G
Total Fat: 24G
(Saturated Fat: 1G)
Fiber: 7G
Sodium: 930MG

1. Heat large covered saucepot of salted water to boiling over high heat. Add linguine and cook as label directs.

2. Meanwhile, in 12-inch skillet, heat 1 tablespoon oil over medium-high heat until hot. Add chicken and salt. Cook for 5 minutes or until chicken is no longer pink throughout, stirring occasionally. Transfer chicken to bowl.

3. To drippings in skillet, add garlic, light parts of green onions, and remaining 1 tablespoon oil; cook for 1 minute. Stir in mushrooms. Cook for 5 minutes or until liquid evaporates. Add cabbage, carrots, and ¼ cup water. Cook for 5 minutes or until vegetables are tender and cabbage wilts.

4. In cup, combine teriyaki sauce and ginger. Drain linguine well; add with teriyaki mixture and chicken to vegetables in skillet. Cook for 2 minutes longer, gently tossing. To serve, sprinkle with reserved dark-green onion tops.

HOW TO: PEEL & GRATE FRESH GINGER

Follow these quick and easy steps to peel and grate this special spice.

PEEL the skin from the portion of gingerroot you'll be using.

GRATE the ginger over a cutting board by holding the root firmly in your hand and moving it back and forth over the smallest holes of a box grater.

Easiest-Ever
SPINACH LASAGNA

What makes this recipe so easy? The slow cooker! Just don't peek inside. Keep the lid on until the end of cooking. Even one quick look will increase the cooking time.

ACTIVE TIME → 10 MINUTES   SLOW-COOK TIME → 4 HOURS   MAKES → 8 SERVINGS

INGREDIENTS

1 container (15 ounces) part-skim ricotta cheese

1 package (10 ounces) frozen chopped spinach, thawed and squeezed dry

8 ounces shredded mozzarella cheese (2 cups)

1 large egg, lightly beaten

¼ teaspoon salt

1 jar (32 ounces) marinara sauce

1 box (9 ounces) no-boil lasagna noodles

EACH SERVING

Calories: About 355
Protein: 20G
Carbohydrates: 37G
Total Fat: 14G
(Saturated Fat: 7G)
Fiber: 4G
Sodium: 815MG

1. In large bowl, combine ricotta, spinach, 1 cup mozzarella, egg, and salt.

2. Spray a 6- to 6½-quart slow-cooker bowl with nonstick cooking spray. In bowl, alternately layer marinara sauce, noodles, and ricotta mixture, starting and ending with marinara sauce and breaking noodles to fit. Top with remaining 1 cup mozzarella.

3. Cover slow cooker with lid and cook as manufacturer directs on low for 4 hours or until noodles are tender.

HOW TO: THAW & SQUEEZE DRY FROZEN SPINACH

This technique also works for cooked fresh spinach.

UNWRAP the frozen spinach and place in a microwave-safe bowl.

MICROWAVE the spinach on High for 1 to 2 minutes or until soft.

LINE a colander with a double thickness of paper towels.

WRAP the spinach in paper towels and squeeze out the excess liquid. (Be sure to do this over the colander in case the paper towel tears.)

Tomato Soup
MAC 'N' CHEESE

Having friends over? This is the recipe for you. Everything can be made ahead through step 4; just cover the ramekins with foil and refrigerate overnight. When ready to serve, bake uncovered for 45 minutes.

ACTIVE TIME → 5 MINUTES   TOTAL TIME → 1 HOUR 15 MINUTES   MAKES → 8 SERVINGS

INGREDIENTS

1 pound cavatappi pasta

4 tablespoons unsalted butter

¼ cup all-purpose flour

2½ cups whole milk

¼ teaspoon salt

1 pound American cheese, chopped

1½ cups marinara sauce

2 tablespoons tomato paste

2 tablespoons plain dried bread crumbs

EACH SERVING

Calories: About 545
Protein: 20G
Carbohydrates: 59G
Total Fat: 25G
(Saturated Fat: 14G)
Fiber: 3G
Sodium: 1,130MG

1. Preheat oven to 375°F. Line rimmed baking sheet with foil.

2. Heat large covered saucepot of water to boiling over high heat. Add cavatappi; cook for 5 minutes. Drain well.

3. Meanwhile, in 5- to 6-quart saucepot, melt butter over medium heat. Sprinkle flour over butter. Cook for 1 minute, stirring. Slowly whisk in milk until smooth. Add salt. Heat to boiling over high heat, whisking often. Reduce heat to medium. Simmer for 2 minutes or until slightly thickened, stirring occasionally.

4. Reduce heat to medium-low. Gradually stir in cheese by handful until smooth, letting cheese melt before adding next batch. Whisk in marinara sauce and tomato paste. Add cavatappi; toss to coat well.

5. Place ramekins on prepared pan. Transfer mixture to eight (8-ounce) ramekins; top with bread crumbs. Spray crumbs with nonstick cooking spray.

6. Bake for 30 to 35 minutes or until sauce is bubbling and crumbs are golden.

Corkscrews with
CHEESE, TOMATOES & PEAS

Colorful veggies rev up the flavor—and nutrients!—of this speedy pasta dish.

ACTIVE TIME → 10 MINUTES   **TOTAL TIME** → 20 MINUTES   **MAKES** → 4 SERVINGS

INGREDIENTS

12 ounces cavatappi pasta

1 package (10 ounces) frozen peas

1 tablespoon butter

2 tablespoons all-purpose flour

¼ teaspoon salt

¼ teaspoon ground black pepper

2 cups low-fat (2%) milk

4 ounces extra-sharp cheddar cheese, shredded (½ cup)

½ cup grated pecorino cheese plus additional for serving

2 medium tomatoes, chopped

2 tablespoons snipped fresh chives

EACH SERVING

Calories: About 640
Protein: 30G
Carbohydrates: 86G
Total Fat: 19G
(Saturated Fat: 10G)
Fiber: 6G
Sodium: 750MG

1. Heat large covered saucepot of salted water to boiling over high heat. Add cavatappi and cook as label directs, adding peas to saucepot for 1 minute before pasta is done.

2. Meanwhile, in 4-quart saucepan, melt butter over medium heat. With wire whisk, stir in flour, salt, and pepper until smooth. Cook for 1 minute, stirring constantly. Gradually whisk in milk; heat to boiling over medium-high heat, stirring constantly. Boil for 1 minute. Remove saucepan from heat; stir in cheddar and ½ cup pecorino until smooth.

3. Drain pasta and peas well; stir into saucepan with cheese mixture until coated. Top with tomatoes and chives. Serve with pecorino.

SMART CHEF! Can't find cavatappi for this recipe (or our Tomato Soup Mac 'N' Cheese, page 115)? Substitute it with another medium-shaped pasta like penne, rotini, or farfalle.

117

FUN FOOD!

PERFECT
CORN!

Make our basic steamed corn, pick a topping, and then nibble away!

ACTIVE TIME → 10 MINUTES   TOTAL TIME → 20 MINUTES   MAKES → 8 SERVINGS

INGREDIENTS
8 ears corn
choice of toppings

1. With large knife, cut off the stalk end from each ear of corn. Arrange 4 ears on large microwave-safe plate. Microwave on High for 30 to 60 seconds or until husk and silk (the strings inside the husk) peel off easily. Repeat with remaining corn.

2. Meanwhile, in large saucepot, bring 3 inches of water to boiling over high heat.

3. Add corn and return to boiling. Reduce heat to low. Cover and simmer for 5 minutes or until tender. Drain. Spread with topping, as desired.

Cilantro-Lime Butter

In food processor with knife blade attached, pulse **6 tablespoons butter,
softened**; **¼ cup packed fresh cilantro leaves**; **¼ cup packed fresh parsley
leaves**; and **1 tablespoon fresh lime juice** until smooth. Transfer mixture to
small bowl and spread evenly over corn.

EACH SERVING: About 165 Calories, 3G Protein, 19G Carbohydrate, 10G Total Fat
(5G Saturated), 2G Fiber, 85MG Sodium

Bruschetta

In medium bowl, mix **2 medium very-ripe tomatoes**, coarsely grated; **2
tablespoons grated Parmesan cheese; 2 tablespoons chopped fresh basil;**
and **¼ teaspoon salt.** Spoon evenly over corn.

EACH SERVING: About 100 Calories, 3G Protein, 20G Carbohydrate, 1G Total Fat
(0G Saturated), 20G Fiber, 112MG Sodium

Taco-Style

In medium microwave-safe bowl, combine **4 tablespoons butter, 2
teaspoons chili powder, 1 teaspoon ground cumin, ¼ teaspoon garlic
powder, and ¼ teaspoon salt.** Cover with vented plastic wrap and microwave
on High 20 to 30 seconds or until butter melts. Stir to combine. Drizzle
evenly over corn using small spoon.

EACH SERVING: About 140 Calories, 3G Protein, 19G Carbohydrate, 7G Total Fat
(4G Saturated), 2G Fiber, 153MG Sodium

Cheesy Garlic-Bacon

In medium bowl, combine **¾ cup garlic-and-herb spreadable cheese** (about
one 5-ounce package), softened. For coating, mix **4 strips bacon**, cooked and
crumbled; and **¼ cup snipped fresh chives.** Spread cheese evenly over corn
and sprinkle with bacon mixture.

EACH SERVING: About 160 Calories, 5G Protein, 20G Carbohydrate, 8G Total Fat
(3G Saturated), 2G Fiber, 131MG Sodium

Asian Sesame
ZUCCHINI NOODLES

If you're crazy for noodles, you're going to love these zesty *zoo*-dles!

TOTAL TIME → 15 MINUTES   MAKES → 4 SIDE-DISH SERVINGS

INGREDIENTS

¼ cup packed fresh cilantro, finely chopped

3 tablespoons seasoned rice vinegar

1 tablespoon toasted sesame oil

2 garlic cloves, crushed with press

¼ teaspoon crushed red pepper, optional

2 teaspoons sugar

½ teaspoon salt

3 medium zucchini, spiralized

EACH SERVING

Calories: About 85
Protein: 2G
Carbohydrates: 12G
Total Fat: 4G
(Saturated Fat: 1G)
Fiber: 2G
Sodium: 575MG

1. In large bowl with wire whisk, mix cilantro, vinegar, oil, garlic, crushed red pepper (if using), sugar, and salt. Add zucchini; toss until well combined. Serve immediately.

WHAT IS IT?

A **SPIRALIZER** is a nifty gadget that turns fresh veggies into noodles. Most models work like a giant pencil sharpener. A feed tube or clamp holds any veggie firmly in place. By using a hand crank, you're able to run the veggie through a perforated metal disk, which transforms the veggie into long, gently curled noodles. If you don't own a spiralizer, you can pick up a handheld julienne slicer at the supermarket or specialty food store.

FUN FOOD!

Three
SUPER SIDES

These veggie sides pair well with any
main dish—and they're scrumptious!
All recipes serve 4.

Sesame Green Beans

In 4-quart saucepan, combine 7 cups water and **1 teaspoon salt**; heat to boiling over high heat. Add **1 pound green beans**, trimmed; heat to boiling. Cover and cook for 6 to 8 minutes or until just tender-crisp. Drain; return green beans to saucepan. Add **1 tablespoon soy sauce**; ½ teaspoon **Asian sesame oil**, and 1½ teaspoons grated, peeled fresh ginger. Reduce heat to low. Cook for about 3 minutes or until flavors have blended, stirring occasionally. Sprinkle with 1½ **teaspoons sesame seeds**, toasted.

EACH SERVING: About 45 Calories, 2G Protein, 8G Carbohydrate, 1G Total Fat (0G Saturated), 3G Fiber, 553MG Sodium

Candied Carrots

Cut **1 pound carrots** in half, then cut thicker pieces in half lengthwise. In 4-quart saucepan, heat 1 inch water to boiling over medium heat. Add carrots and heat to boiling. Reduce heat to low. Cover and simmer for about 15 minutes or until tender. Drain carrots and return to saucepan. Add **2 tablespoons butter, 3 tablespoons packed brown sugar**, and **1 teaspoon fresh lemon juice**. Increase heat to medium. Cook for about 5 minutes or until sugar has melted and carrots are glazed, stirring gently. Stir in ½ **teaspoon freshly grated lemon peel**.

EACH SERVING: About 135 Calories, 1G Protein, 20G Carbohydrate, 6G Total Fat (4G Saturated), 3G Fiber, 98MG Sodium

Broiled Parmesan Tomatoes

Preheat oven to broil. Cut **4 small ripe plum tomatoes** lengthwise in half and set aside. In 1-quart saucepan, melt **1 tablespoon butter** over low heat. Add **1 garlic clove**, finely chopped. Cook until golden, stirring. Remove pan from heat. Spread ¼ **cup grated Parmesan cheese** on sheet of wax paper. Dip cut side of each tomato half in melted butter mixture, then dip same side into Parmesan. Place tomatoes cheese-side up on rack set in broiling pan. Sprinkle any remaining Parmesan on top and drizzle with any remaining butter mixture. Broil as close to heat source as possible for 3 to 4 minutes or until cheese melts.

EACH SERVING: About 70 Calories, 3G Protein, 4G Carbohydrate, 5G Total Fat (3G Saturated), 1G Fiber, 151MG Sodium

Super-Creamy POTATOES

Half-and-half and good ol' butter are the secrets to these spectacular mashed spuds.
Double the recipe if you're serving a crowd.

ACTIVE TIME → 15 MINUTES   TOTAL TIME → 40 MINUTES   MAKES → 6 SERVINGS

INGREDIENTS

2 pounds Yukon gold
potatoes, peeled and
cut into halves

salt

¾ cup half-and-half
or light cream

3 tablespoons butter,
cut up

EACH SERVING

Calories: About 185
Protein: 3G
Carbohydrates: 27G
Total Fat: 7G
(Saturated Fat: 4G)
Fiber: 2G
Sodium: 344MG

1. In large saucepot, combine potatoes, enough cold water to cover by 1 inch, and 1½ tablespoons salt. Partially cover and heat to simmering over high heat. Uncover and simmer for 20 to 25 minutes or until potatoes are very tender but not falling apart, stirring occasionally.

2. Meanwhile, in 2-cup glass measuring cup, combine half-and-half and butter. Microwave on High for 1 minute or until butter melts.

3. Drain potatoes well; return to empty pot. Mash potatoes or put through ricer. Stir in milk mixture and ½ teaspoon salt.

? WHAT IS IT?

A **RICER** is a nifty tool used for pressing cooked potatoes (or other soft foods) through a bunch of little holes, resulting in rice-like pieces (hence the name). Because air is incorporated into the potato as it's pressed, the ricer gives you the lightest mashed potatoes possible. No lumps guaranteed!

Cheesy
HASSELBACKS

These accordion-like baked taters have extra nooks for melty cheese.
Top them off with sour cream, chives, or crumbled bacon—or all three!

ACTIVE TIME → 20 MINUTES   TOTAL TIME → 55 MINUTES   MAKES → 6 SERVINGS

INGREDIENTS

6 medium russet potatoes

3 tablespoons olive oil

¾ teaspoon salt

4 ounces cheddar cheese, cut into thin sticks

EACH SERVING

Calories: About 305
Protein: 8G
Carbohydrates: 39G
Total Fat: 13G
(Saturated Fat: 4G)
Fiber: 2G
Sodium: 424MG

1. Preheat oven to 425°F.

2. Thinly slice potatoes (but don't cut all the way through). Arrange on rimmed baking sheet. Brush tops with 1½ tablespoons oil.

3. Bake for 30 minutes. Brush tops with remaining 1½ tablespoons oil; sprinkle with salt. Bake for 30 minutes or until tender. Remove potatoes from oven; carefully place cheddar sticks between slices. Bake for 5 minutes longer or until cheese melts.

5

Sweet Treats

Imagine a snake-shaped cake, candy-bar pie, and even "baked" apples that you don't have to bake! Are you more of a cookie person? We have a recipe for the best chocolate-chip cookies and fruity crumb bars you'll ever taste. If ice-cream sandwiches or hot fudgy brownies are on your recipe radar—well, we've got that covered, too. These recipes have the power to satisfy any sweet tooth!

No-Bake
SNAKE CAKE

This serpent has a secret: he's made from puffed-rice cereal treats. Ssssweet!

TOTAL TIME → 2 HOURS (PLUS DECORATING)   MAKES → 12 SERVINGS

INGREDIENTS

4 tablespoons butter

1 bag (10 ounces) miniature marshmallows

1 box (12 ounces) puffed-rice cereal

1 container (16 ounces) caramel frosting

M&M's, strawberry fruit leather, and chocolate wafers, crushed, for decorations

EACH SERVING

Calories: About 300
Protein: 1G
Carbohydrates: 54G
Total Fat: 10G
(Saturated Fat: 4G)
Fiber: 0G
Sodium: 127G

1. Grease 9-inch round springform pan. In large pot over medium heat, melt butter. Add marshmallows, setting 2 aside. Cook for about 3 minutes or until melted, stirring. Remove pot from heat. Add 6 cups cereal to pot, folding until evenly coated.

2. Wait for marshmallow mixture to cool slightly, then press into prepared springform pan. Let cool completely.

3. Remove "cake" from pan. Using any 28-ounce can as guide, cut 4-inch circle from cake's center and set aside. Cut the remaining O shape in half. You should now have two C-shaped pieces

4. On platter, separate and arrange the two pieces into a snake. Slice off sides of cut-out circle to form the head.

5. Frost cake with caramel frosting. Time to decorate! Use marshmallows and M&M's for eyes, strawberry fruit leather for tongue, and chocolate wafers for "dirt."

Cupcake
QUEEN

If you're ready to say yes to the dress, our pretty-in-pink "gown" takes the cake!
Feel free to stray from the directions about decorating in order to design the dress of your dreams.

TOTAL TIME → 1 HOUR (PLUS DECORATING)   MAKES → 27 CUPCAKES

INGREDIENTS

1 box (15¼ ounces)
yellow cake mix

5½ cups confectioners'
sugar

¾ cup butter (1½ sticks),
softened

1½ teaspoons vanilla
extract

6 to 8 tablespoons milk

red liquid food coloring

silver, white, and pink
candy dragées or
nonpareils

tiara and wand, optional

EACH CUPCAKE

Calories: About 240
Protein: 1G
Carbohydrates: 37G
Total Fat: 9G
(Saturated Fat: 4G)
Fiber: 0G
Sodium: 169MG

1. Preheat oven to 350°F. Line twenty-seven 2½-inch muffin-pan cups with paper liners.

2. Make cake mix as label directs. Spoon batter into lined muffin-pan cups. Bake 18 to 23 minutes or until toothpick inserted in centers comes out clean. Cool cupcakes in pans on wire racks for 10 minutes. Remove cupcakes from pans and cool completely on wire racks.

3. In large bowl with mixer at medium-high speed, beat sugar, butter, vanilla, and 6 tablespoons milk until smooth. Beat until frosting is light and fluffy, occasionally scraping bowl with rubber spatula.

4. Add food coloring, one drop at a time, until frosting is tinted pink. Transfer ⅓ cup frosting to small bowl and add more coloring, one drop at a time, until frosting is tinted dark pink.

5. Transfer pink frosting to large piping bag fitted with star tip. Decoratively pipe frosting onto cupcakes.

6. Arrange cupcakes in dress shape on a platter or piece of cardboard.

7. Fill small piping bag with dark-pink frosting and fit with star tip. Pipe "flowers" to fill in gaps between cupcakes. Decorate flower shapes with silver dragées. Arrange silver, white, and pink dragées to make a "belt." Add tiara and wand for a decorative flair, if using.

Peanut
BUTTER CUP PIE

Sweet, salty, and oh-so yummy, this candy bar–inspired pie is also a cinch to make.

ACTIVE TIME → 15 MINUTES   **TOTAL TIME →** 20 MINUTES (PLUS CHILLING)   **MAKES →** 12 SERVINGS

INGREDIENTS

8 ounces milk chocolate, chopped

1 cup heavy cream

1 cup creamy peanut butter

2 cups thin pretzel sticks, broken into pieces

1 (9-inch) ready-made chocolate piecrust

EACH SERVING

Calories: About 380
Protein: 8G
Carbohydrates: 31G
Total Fat: 26G
(Saturated Fat: 10G)
Fiber: 3G
Sodium: 218MG

1. In 2-quart saucepan, combine chocolate and ½ cup cream. Cook over low heat for 4 to 5 minutes or until chocolate melts, stirring. Pour half of chocolate into medium-size bowl; set aside.

2. Remove saucepan from heat. Stir in peanut butter until blended. Cool completely.

3. In another large bowl with mixer on medium-high speed, beat remaining ½ cup cream until stiff peaks form (i.e., when you remove the beater from the cream and it stays firm, without losing its shape).

4. With rubber spatula, fold whipped cream and 1 cup pretzels into peanut-butter mixture until blended. Spread in piecrust. Spread reserved chocolate mixture on top; cover evenly with remaining 1 cup pretzels. Refrigerate for 4 hours or until firm.

HOW TO: USE A MIXER

When using this nifty contraption, remember:

NEVER put your hands in the mixing bowl when the mixer is on.

EVEN on low speed, a mixer is fast. When adding dry ingredients, do so gradually so they don't splash out of the bowl.

BEFORE scraping ingredients down the side of the mixing bowl, turn off the mixer and wait for the beaters to come to a complete stop.

DON'T remove the beaters until you turn off the mixer and unplug it.

Crispy
CHOCOLATE-CHIP COOKIES

If you like your chocolate-chip cookies with a butterscotch flavor and an airy crunch, this recipe is for you.

ACTIVE TIME → 20 MINUTES   TOTAL TIME → 40 MINUTES (PLUS CHILLING)
MAKES → ABOUT 4 DOZEN COOKIES

INGREDIENTS

1⅔ cups all-purpose flour

1 teaspoon baking soda

1 teaspoon salt

1 cup unsalted butter (2 sticks)

1 cup firmly packed brown sugar

½ cup granulated sugar

2 teaspoons vanilla extract

1 large egg

1 bag (12 ounces) semisweet chocolate chips

EACH COOKIE

Calories: About 110
Protein: 1G
Carbohydrates: 14G
Total Fat: 6G
(Saturated Fat: 3G)
Fiber: 0G
Sodium: 78MG

1. In large bowl with wire whisk, mix flour, baking soda, and salt.

2. In another large bowl with mixer on medium-high speed, beat butter and sugars for 5 minutes or until very light and fluffy. Beat in 1 tablespoon water and vanilla. Beat in egg until combined. Reduce speed to low; gradually beat in flour mixture just until blended. Stir in chocolate chips.

3. Transfer dough to zip-seal plastic bag; squeeze out air and seal bag. Refrigerate for at least 24 hours, or up to 72 hours.

4. Preheat oven to 350°F. Line two large cookie sheets with parchment paper.

5. With 1½-inch-wide cookie scoop, scoop chilled dough 2 inches apart on prepared cookie sheets. Bake cookies for 10 to 12 minutes or until edges and centers are browned. Slide cookies, still on parchment, onto wire racks to cool completely. Repeat with remaining dough and cooled, newly lined cookie sheets.

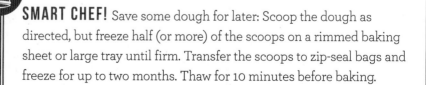

SMART CHEF! Save some dough for later: Scoop the dough as directed, but freeze half (or more) of the scoops on a rimmed baking sheet or large tray until firm. Transfer the scoops to zip-seal bags and freeze for up to two months. Thaw for 10 minutes before baking.

Chocolate Volcano
COOKIES

Crunchy on the outside and chewy on the inside, customize these cookies with your favorite chips (milk chocolate, or dark chocolate, or peanut butter, or . . .).

ACTIVE TIME → 10 MINUTES   **TOTAL TIME →** 45 MINUTES   **MAKES →** ABOUT 2 DOZEN COOKIES

INGREDIENTS

1 package (16 ounces) confectioners' sugar

¾ cup unsweetened cocoa

½ teaspoon salt

4 large egg whites

1 tablespoon vanilla extract

1½ cups semisweet or bittersweet chocolate chips

EACH COOKIE

Calories: About 135
Protein: 2G
Carbohydrates: 27G
Total Fat: 4G
(Saturated Fat: 2G)
Fiber: 2G
Sodium: 60MG

1. Preheat oven to 350°F. Line two large cookie sheets with parchment paper; lightly coat paper with nonstick cooking spray.

2. In large bowl with wire whisk, mix confectioners' sugar, cocoa, and salt. Add egg whites and vanilla; stir with wooden spoon until smooth. Fold in chocolate chips. Set dough aside for 5 minutes.

3. Drop dough by rounded tablespoonfuls 2 inches apart on prepared cookie sheets. Bake for 13 to 15 minutes or until set and crackly. Cool for 3 minutes on cookie sheets on wire racks; with metal spatula, carefully transfer cookies to wire racks to cool completely.

?

WHAT IS IT?

A stainless-steel **COOKIE SCOOP** portions equal mounds of dough onto a cookie sheet. This way, you get perfectly shaped cookies every time.

Maine Blueberry
CRUMB BARS

These berry-topped streusel squares taste like mini blueberry pies.
For extra crunch, add ¼ cup old-fashioned oats to the topping.

ACTIVE TIME → 20 MINUTES   TOTAL TIME → 1 HOUR 30 MINUTES   MAKES → 1½ DOZEN BARS

INGREDIENTS

1 lemon

2½ cups all-purpose flour

¾ cup granulated sugar

1 teaspoon ground cinnamon

½ teaspoon salt

1 cup (2 sticks) butter, cut up and chilled

2 teaspoons vanilla extract

4 cups fresh blueberries

½ cup packed brown sugar

2 tablespoons cornstarch

EACH BAR

Calories: About 235
Protein: 2G
Carbohydrates: 34G
Total Fat: 11G
(Saturated Fat: 7G)
Fiber: 1G
Sodium: 140MG

1. Preheat oven to 375°F. Line 13-by-9-inch baking pan with enough foil to fold over rim. Spray foil with nonstick cooking spray.

2. From lemon, grate 1 teaspoon peel and squeeze 2 tablespoons juice.

3. In food processor with knife blade attached, pulse flour, granulated sugar, cinnamon, lemon peel, and salt until combined. Add butter and vanilla. Pulse just until dough resembles crumbs. Transfer half of dough to prepared pan. Place remaining dough in refrigerator. Firmly press dough in pan into even layer. Bake for 15 minutes.

4. Meanwhile, in large bowl, toss blueberries, brown sugar, cornstarch, and lemon juice.

5. After taking crust out of oven, spread berry mixture over crust. Firmly squeeze chilled dough into small clumps and scatter all over berries. Bake for 50 minutes to 1 hour or until topping is golden brown. Cool completely in pan on wire rack. Cut into squares. Bars can be made ahead, wrapped in plastic, and refrigerated up to 1 day.

SMART CHEF! To make sure the cut-up butter is super-cold for this recipe, stick it in the freezer for 10 minutes before making the dough in step 3.

Cocoa BROWNIES

Once you try these easy-peasy brownies, you'll never go back to the boxed stuff.

ACTIVE TIME → 15 MINUTES   **TOTAL TIME →** 35 MINUTES (PLUS COOLING)   **MAKES →** 16 BROWNIES

INGREDIENTS

½ cup all-purpose flour

½ cup unsweetened cocoa

¼ teaspoon baking powder

¼ teaspoon salt

6 tablespoons butter

1 cup sugar

2 large eggs

2 teaspoons vanilla extract

⅓ cup mini chocolate chips, optional

EACH BROWNIE

Calories: About 120
Protein: 2G
Carbohydrates: 17G
Total Fat: 6G
(Saturated Fat: 3G)
Fiber: 1G
Sodium: 100MG

1. Preheat oven to 350°F. Grease 8 x 8-inch metal baking pan. In medium bowl with wire whisk, mix flour, cocoa, baking powder, and salt.

2. In 3-quart saucepan, melt butter over low heat. Remove saucepan from heat; with spatula, stir in sugar; eggs, one at a time; and vanilla until well blended. Stir in flour mixture. Spread batter in prepared baking pan. Sprinkle with chocolate chips, if using.

3. Bake for 18 to 20 minutes or until toothpick inserted in brownies 2 inches from center comes out almost clean. Cool brownies completely in pan on wire rack.

4. When cool, cut brownies into 4 strips, then cut each strip crosswise into 4 squares.

SMART CHEF! If a few moist crumbs cling to the toothpick in step 3, the brownies are done.

Cute Little
CHEESECAKES

These poppers are irresistible!

ACTIVE TIME 4 → 30 MINUTES   TOTAL TIME → 1 HOUR (PLUS COOLING)   MAKES → 2 DOZEN CHEESECAKES

INGREDIENTS

CRUST

1 sleeve graham crackers
(about 9 crackers)

2 teaspoons sugar

¼ teaspoon salt

4 tablespoons butter,
melted

FILLING

2 packages (8 ounces each)
cream cheese, softened

1 cup sugar

2 teaspoons vanilla extract

⅛ teaspoon salt

3 large eggs

¼ cup heavy cream

raspberries and mint
sprigs, for garnish

EACH CHEESECAKE

Calories: About 75
Protein: 1G
Carbohydrates: 7G
Total Fat: 5G
(Saturated Fat: 3G)
Fiber: 0G
Sodium: 60MG

1. **Prepare Crust:** Preheat oven to 350°F. Line 48 miniature muffin-pan cups with paper liners.

2. In food processor with knife blade attached, pulse graham crackers, sugar, and salt until finely ground. Add butter; pulse until mixture resembles wet sand. Press about 1 heaping teaspoon crumb mixture into bottom of each liner. Bake for 5 minutes or until pale golden. Cool completely on wire racks. Reduce oven temperature to 325°F.

3. **Prepare Filling:** In large bowl with mixer on medium speed, beat cream cheese and sugar for 3 minutes or until light and fluffy. Beat in vanilla and salt until combined. Add eggs 1 at a time, beating well after each addition. Beat in cream. Divide filling among prepared liners.

4. Bake for 12 to 15 minutes or until filling is set but still slightly jiggly and moist in center. Let cool in pans on wire racks for 5 minutes; transfer cheesecakes to wire racks to cool completely. Garnish with raspberries and mint sprigs.

Home-Style
BANANA BREAD

When life gives you (overripe) bananas, make banana bread!

ACTIVE TIME → 20 MINUTES   **TOTAL TIME →** 1 HOUR 20 MINUTES (PLUS COOLING)   **MAKES →** 16 SERVINGS

INGREDIENTS

2 cups all-purpose flour

¾ teaspoon baking soda

½ teaspoon salt

2 cups mashed very ripe bananas (4 medium)

1 teaspoon vanilla extract

½ cup butter (1 stick), softened

½ cup granulated sugar

½ cup packed brown sugar

2 large eggs

EACH SERVING

Calories: About 200
Protein: 3G
Carbohydrates: 32G
Total Fat: 7G
(Saturated Fat: 4G)
Fiber: 1G
Sodium: 205MG

1. Preheat oven to 325°F. Grease 8½-by-4½-inch metal loaf pan. In medium bowl with wire whisk, mix flour, baking soda, and salt. In small bowl, combine bananas and vanilla until blended.

2. In large bowl with mixer on medium speed, beat butter and sugars until light and fluffy. Beat in eggs 1 at a time. Reduce speed to low; alternately add flour mixture and banana mixture, beginning and ending with flour mixture and occasionally scraping bowl with rubber spatula. Beat batter just until blended.

3. Pour batter into prepared pan. Bake about 1 hour, until toothpick inserted in center comes out clean. Cool loaf in pan on wire rack 10 minutes; remove from pan and cool completely on wire rack before slicing.

Homemade Fudgy
ICE-CREAM SANDWICHES

These ultimate sandwiches pair ice cream (the flavor is your pick)
with cookies that stay chewy—even when frozen.

ACTIVE TIME → 30 MINUTES   TOTAL TIME → 50 MINUTES (PLUS FREEZING)   MAKES → 1 DOZEN SANDWICHES

INGREDIENTS

½ cup (1 stick) butter,
at room temperature
and cut up

1 bag (12 ounces)
semisweet chocolate
chips

1 can (14 ounces)
sweetened condensed
milk

¼ teaspoon salt

1 cup all-purpose flour

1 tablespoon vanilla
extract

2 pints ice cream of
choice, slightly softened

EACH ICE-CREAM SANDWICH

Calories: About 425
Protein: 6G
Carbohydrates: 53G
Total Fat: 22G
(Saturated Fat: 13G)
Fiber: 0G
Sodium: 177MG

1. Preheat oven to 350°F. Line two large cookie sheets with parchment paper.

2. In 4-quart saucepan, combine butter, chocolate chips, condensed milk, and salt. Cook over medium-low heat for 5 to 6 minutes or until melted, stirring. Remove pan from heat. Stir in flour and vanilla until combined.

3. With 1½-inch-wide cookie scoop, scoop dough 2 inches apart on prepared cookie sheets. Flatten slightly. Bake 8 to 10 minutes or until tops are dry but still soft when pressed.

4. Cool cookies on cookie sheets on wire racks for 5 minutes. With spatula, transfer cookies to wire racks to cool completely. Repeat with remaining batter if necessary.

5. Press 1 small scoop ice cream between 2 cookies. Freeze sandwiches 1 hour or until firm.

SMART CHEF! Once the ice-cream sandwiches are firm, enjoy them right away, or wrap each sandwich in plastic wrap and freeze in a zip-close freezer bag for up to 2 weeks.

Watermelon
PIZZA

Celebrate the Fourth of July with this fruity, patriotic "pie."

TOTAL TIME → 15 MINUTES   MAKES → 4 SERVINGS

INGREDIENTS

2 cups ricotta cheese

1 package (8 ounces) cream cheese, softened

¼ cup honey

2 teaspoons vanilla extract

4 (1-inch-thick) slices seedless watermelon

2 cups assorted berries

½ cup sweetened coconut flakes, toasted

fresh mint sprigs, for garnish

EACH SERVING

Calories: About 170
Protein: 8G
Carbohydrates: 16G
Total Fat: 14G
(Saturated Fat: 9G)
Fiber: 1G
Sodium: 105MG

1. In large bowl, combine ricotta, cream cheese, honey, and vanilla; stir with wooden spoon until blended.

2. Spread ¾ cup cheese mixture on each watermelon slice; sprinkle each with ½ cup berries and 2 tablespoons coconut. Garnish slices with mint sprigs.

SMART CHEF! To toast coconut, spread it on a small microwave-safe plate. Microwave on High, in 30-second intervals, for 1½ to 2 minutes or until beginning to turn golden, stirring between intervals. Cool completely.

Fudgy Waffle
BROWNIES

Waffles with store-bought brownie mix are often hard and crunchy, so we created this recipe for those who prefer their waffles soft. The texture is terrific!

ACTIVE TIME → 20 MINUTES   TOTAL TIME → 35 MINUTES   MAKES → 12 SERVINGS

INGREDIENTS

6 tablespoons butter, cut up

1 bar (35 ounces) bittersweet chocolate, chopped

¾ cup sugar

1 large egg, beaten

2 teaspoons vanilla extract

½ cup whole milk

1 cup all-purpose flour

¼ cup unsweetened cocoa

2 teaspoons baking powder

½ teaspoon salt

1 cup butterscotch, peanut butter, or chocolate chips

ice cream and berries, optional

EACH SERVING

Calories: About 280
Protein: 5G
Carbohydrates: 35G
Total Fat: 14G
(Saturated Fat: 8G)
Fiber: 2G
Sodium: 290MG

1. Preheat oven to 225°F. Preheat waffle maker.

2. In 4-quart saucepan, combine butter and chocolate. Cook over medium-low heat for 2 to 3 minutes or until melted and smooth, stirring. Remove pan from heat. Stir in sugar. Whisk in egg and vanilla until combined. Stir in milk.

3. In medium bowl with wire whisk, mix flour, cocoa, baking powder, and salt. Stir flour mixture into butter mixture just until smooth. Fold in chips.

4. Spray waffle maker with nonstick cooking spray. Pour ⅓ to ½ cup batter onto heated waffle maker. Close waffle maker; cook for 2 to 3 minutes or until just set and crisp around edges. With edge of thin silicone spatula, cut brownie into quarters and gently lift each quarter from waffle maker. Place waffle directly on oven rack to keep warm. Repeat with remaining batter. Serve with ice cream and berries, if using.

Micro-Baked Apples
WITH DRIED CHERRIES

Grab a few apples and—voilà!
You've got a comfort-dessert classic in less than 30 minutes.

ACTIVE TIME → 5 MINUTES   TOTAL TIME → 20 MINUTES (PLUS STANDING)   MAKES → 4 SERVINGS

INGREDIENTS

4 large Fuji or Gala
apples (8 ounces each)

4 teaspoons butter

4 tablespoons dried
cherries

1 teaspoon sugar

¼ teaspoon apple
pie spice

¼ cup walnuts,
chopped, optional

EACH SERVING

Calories: About 150
Protein: 1G
Carbohydrates: 32G
Total Fat: 4G
(Saturated Fat: 1G)
Fiber: 5G
Sodium: 50MG

1. With apple corer, core apples, but don't cut through to bottoms. Beginning at stem end, peel apples one-third of the way down. Stand apples in 8-by-8-inch glass baking dish or 9-inch glass pie plate. Fill center of each apple with 1 teaspoon butter, 1 tablespoon dried cherries, and 1 teaspoon water.

2. In cup, combine sugar and apple pie spice; sprinkle over apples in dish. Cover with waxed paper. Microwave on Medium-High (70 percent power) for 14 minutes or until apples are very tender when tested with fork.

3. Let apples stand, covered, 5 minutes. Sprinkle with walnuts, if using.

INDEX

Note: Page numbers in italics indicate photos on pages separate from recipes.

PHOTO CREDITS

METRIC CONVERSION CHARTS

The recipes that appear in this cookbook use the standard United States method for measuring liquid and dry or solid ingredients (teaspoons, tablespoons, and cups). The information on this chart is provided to help cooks outside the U.S. successfully use these recipes. All equivalents are approximate.

METRIC EQUIVALENTS FOR DIFFERENT TYPES OF INGREDIENTS

STANDARD CUP	FINE POWDER (e.g. flour)	GRAIN (e.g. rice)	GRANULAR (e.g. sugar)	LIQUID SOLIDS (e.g. butter)	LIQUID (e.g. milk)
¾	105 g	113 g	143 g	150 g	180 ml
⅔	93 g	100 g	125 g	133 g	160 ml
½	70 g	75 g	95 g	100 g	120 ml
⅓	47 g	50 g	63 g	67 g	80 ml
¼	35 g	38 g	48 g	50 g	60 ml
⅛	18 g	19 g	24 g	25 g	30 ml

USEFUL EQUIVALENTS FOR LIQUID INGREDIENTS BY VOLUME

¼ tsp	=						1 ml
½ tsp	=						2 ml
1 tsp	=						5 ml
3 tsp	=	1 Tbsp	=		½ fl oz	=	15 ml
		2 Tbsp	=	⅛ cup	=	1 fl oz	=	30 ml
		4 Tbsp	=	¼ cup	=	2 fl oz	=	60 ml
		5⅓ Tbsp	=	⅓ cup	=	3 fl oz	=	80 ml
		8 Tbsp	=	½ cup	=	4 fl oz	=	120 ml
		10⅔ Tbsp	=	⅔ cup	=	5 fl oz	=	160 ml
		12 Tbsp	=	¾ cup	=	6 fl oz	=	180 ml
		16 Tbsp	=	1 cup	=	8 fl oz	=	240 ml
		1 pt	=	2 cups	=	16 fl oz	=	480 ml
		1 qt	=	4 cups	=	32 fl oz	=	960 ml
						33 fl oz	=	1000 ml= 1 L

USEFUL EQUIVALENTS FOR DRY INGREDIENTS BY WEIGHT

(To convert ounces to grams, multiply the number of ounces by 30.)

1 oz	=	¹⁄₁₆ lb	=	30 g
4 oz	=	¼ lb	=	120 g
8 oz	=	½ lb	=	240 g
12 oz	=	¾ lb	=	360 g
16 oz	=	1 lb	=	480 g

USEFUL EQUIVALENTS FOR COOKING/OVEN TEMPERATURES

	Fahrenheit	Celsius	Gas Mark
Freeze Water	32° F	0° C	
Room Temperature	68° F	20° C	
Boil Water	212° F	100° C	
Bake	325° F	160° C	3
	350° F	180° C	4
	375° F	190° C	5
	400° F	200° C	6
	425° F	220° C	7
	450° F	230° C	8
Broil			Grill

USEFUL EQUIVALENTS LENGTH

(To convert inches to centimeters, multiply the number of inches by 2.5.)

1 in	=					2.5 cm	
6 in	=	½ ft	=			15 cm	
12 in	=	1 ft	=			30 cm	
36 in	=	3 ft	=	1 yd	=	90 cm	
40 in	=					100 cm	=	1 m

GOOD HOUSEKEEPING
TRIPLE TEST PROMISE

At *Good Housekeeping*, we want to make sure that every recipe we print works in any oven, with any brand of ingredient, no matter what. That's why, in our test kitchens at the Good Housekeeping Research Institute, we go all out: We test each recipe at least three times—and, often, several more times after that.

When a recipe is first developed, one member of our team prepares the dish, and we judge it on these criteria: It must be delicious, family-friendly, healthy, and easy to make.

1 The recipe is then tested several more times to fine-tune the flavor and ease of preparation, always by the same team member, using the same equipment.

2 Next, another team member follows the recipe as written, varying the brands of ingredients and kinds of equipment. Even the types of stoves we use are changed.

3 A third team member repeats the whole process using yet another set of equipment and alternative ingredients. By the time the recipes appear on these pages, they are guaranteed to work in any kitchen, including yours. We promise.

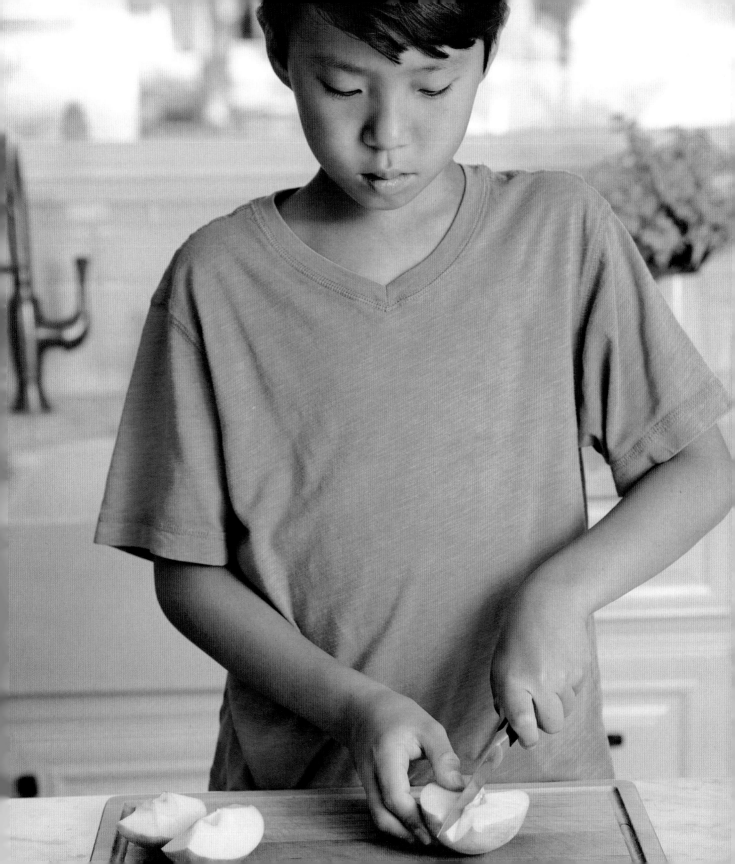

HEARSTBOOKS

An Imprint of Sterling Publishing Co., Inc.
1166 Avenue of the Americas
New York, NY 10036

GOOD HOUSEKEEPING is a registered trademark of Hearst Magazine Media, Inc.

ISBN 978-1-61837-240-6

The Good Housekeeping Cookbook Seal guarantees that the recipes in this cookbook meet the strict standards
of the Good Housekeeping Research Institute. The Institute has been a source of reliable information and a consumer advocate since
1900, and established its seal of approval in 1909. Every recipe has been triple-tested for ease, reliability, and great taste.

Distributed in Canada by Sterling Publishing Co., Inc.
c/o Canadian Manda Group, 664 Annette Street
Toronto, Ontario, M6S 2C8, Canada
Distributed in Australia by NewSouth Books
University of New South Wales, Sydney, NSW 2052, Australia

For information about custom editions, special sales, and premium and corporate purchases,
please contact Sterling Special Sales at 800-805-5489 or specialsales@sterlingpublishing.com.

Manufactured in China

Lot#:

12 14 16 15 13 11

04/21

goodhousekeeping.com

sterlingpublishing.com

Book design by Heather Kelly

GOOD HOUSEKEEPING

Jane Francisco
EDITOR IN CHIEF
Melissa Geurts
DESIGN DIRECTOR
Susan Westmoreland
FOOD DIRECTOR
Sharon Franke
KITCHEN APPLIANCES & TECHNOLOGY DIRECTOR
THE GOOD HOUSEKEEPING INSTITUTE